WHAT IS NEXT FOR MALI?
THE ROOTS OF CONFLICT
AND CHALLENGES TO STABILITY

The United States strongly condemns the violence initiated by elements of the armed forces of Mali. We call for the immediate restoration of constitutional rule in Mali, including full civilian authority over the armed forces and respect for the country's democratic institutions. . . .

The White House
March 2012[1]

What have you got to say my friends
About this painful time we are living through?

Lyrics from the song,
Imidiwan Ma Tennam,
by the Tuareg-Berber band,
Tinariwen, 2011[2]

INTRODUCTION

At first glance, the descent of Mali into chaos appears swift and sudden. Mali had often been described as a model of democracy and stability on the continent. Long recognized for its cultural richness embodied in ancient cities such as Timbuktu, Mali is also a close ally of the United States and an important participant in Global War on Terror[3] (GWOT) efforts to counter terrorism and improve security in the Sahel region. In February 2012, Mali hosted the Atlas Accord, an annual joint U.S.-Mali military exercise that focused on improved air drop capabilities to effectively deliver military resupply materials and humanitarian aid.[4]

Just a few weeks later, on March 22, members of the Malian military, led by a U.S.-trained soldier, Cap-

tain Amadou Sanogo, overthrew Mali's democratical-
ly-led civilian government. At the time, northern Mali
was already deeply embroiled in a long-running conflict between the Tuareg ethnic minority and the government. Indeed, frustration at the lack of sufficient
central government support in the military campaign
against the Tuareg rebels was a major justification cit-
ed by the coup leaders for their actions. The coup and
the ongoing Tuareg rebellion created a severe security
vacuum in Mali's northern provinces. Al-Qaeda in the
Islamic Maghreb (AQIM), which had been expanding
its reach in the Sahel over the last decade, was quick to
capitalize on the void and occupied the north's major
cities. Waves of refugees fled; those who stayed faced
life under harsh interpretations of sharia, or Islamic
law, imposed by AQIM and allied groups such as
Ansar Dine.

With Mali's democratically elected government
overthrown, French troops, under the auspices of a
United Nations Security Council Resolution (UNSCR),
initiated combat operations against Islamist militants
in the country's remote northern region in January 2013.[5] In less than a month, Operation SERVAL
forced AQIM and allied groups out of the region's cities, clearing the way for an African-led International
Support Mission to Mali (AFISMA) organized by the
Economic Community of West African States (ECOW-
AS) and the potential return of democratic rule to the
country as a whole.

Though events in Mali have moved quickly over
the last year, and indeed continue to do so, the underlying causes of the current crisis are long-standing.
The dissatisfaction of the Tuaregs, the legacies of colonial rule, and geographic realities are by no means
new developments. However, more recent events

have served to catalyze simmering issues into active conflict. The political and security instability created by the overthrow of Muammar Gaddafi's regime in Libya and the coup d'etat that ousted Malian president Amadou Toumani Touré, for example, emboldened an array of actors, including Tuareg rebels with nationalist causes, criminals, and various groups of Islamic militants.

The interrelated security challenges Mali faces today are complex, summed up by David Lewis as "a toxic cocktail of rebels, weapons, refugees, drought, smugglers, and violent Islamic militants."[6] While the transnational threat posed by AQIM and affiliated groups is of deepest concern to the United States and its European allies, violent extremism is only one of a number of issues destabilizing Mali's security. Given the interconnected nature of these challenges, policies and security frameworks that follow the French intervention must take a broad and comprehensive approach to security and stability in Mali that goes well beyond the provision of physical security.

Legal restrictions prevented the United States from providing direct military aid to Mali after March 2012 because that government seized power in a coup.[7] The United States provided intelligence and air logistical support to the French military operation. Three KC-135 tankers were used to refuel French jet fighters and bombers, and the United States provided airlift to transport a French mechanized infantry to Mali.[8] It seems likely the U.S. role in Mali, and in the region overall, will increase. In January 2013, the United States signed a status of forces agreement with neighboring Niger, a move that could pave the way for a possible U.S. drone base. Niger is also the focus for the development of an intelligence hub by both the United

States and the French.[9] The restoration of democratic rule, through elections scheduled for July 2013, will also enable the United States to resume its foreign aid programs for Mali, some of which were suspended after the March 2012 coup.[10]

With AQIM now rooted out of Mali's northern cities, the current dual challenge for the United States, France, and the broader international community is to craft a policy that will bring long-term stability to a key ally in the fight against violent Islamic extremism in the Sahel and, at the same time, rebuild a regional security framework. While restoring physical security is obviously central to this framework, the underlying complex and overlapping socio-economic and political issues that impact security must also be addressed. This monograph attempts to contribute to the current discussions on the future U.S. policy for Mali by exploring the deeper background to the crisis. Such issues include the long-running grievances of the Tuareg minority, the challenges of uneven development, regional instability wrought by the Arab Spring, and a worsening humanitarian crisis. This monograph will also examine the weaknesses of the regional security framework in place prior to the March 2012 coup and the challenges a new regional security framework will need to overcome to bring effective, long-term security to this crucial region.

Why Mali Matters.

Mali is remote and distant from much of the globe. It is one of the poorest countries in the world. And yet, the situation in Mali and the future of the country will have significant impact at the national, regional, and international levels.

4

Geography is the key to much of Mali's importance. Nestled deep in the interior of West Africa, Mali encompasses over 478,841 square miles (1,240,192 square kilometers [km]),[11] a large territory approximately the size of France or twice the size of Texas in the United States. With only 15.84 million people,[12] Mali is sparsely populated. The north is either desert or semi-arid, and over 90 percent of the population is heavily concentrated in the country's less arid southern half. The capital, Bamako, located on the Niger River, boasts over 1.6 million people and is one of the fastest growing cities in Africa.[13] In the north, though cities such as Gao and Timbuktu loom large in ancient history, they are a fraction of the size of Bamako and host few economic opportunities.

Source: *World Factbook*, Washington, DC: Central Intelligence Agency, August 13, 2013.

Map 1. Mali.

Mali is landlocked and shares long and often permeable borders with seven other states: Algeria (1,376-km, 855 miles), Niger (821-km, 510 miles), Burkina Faso (1,000-km, 621 miles), Côte d'Ivoire (532-km, 330 miles), Guinea (858-km, 533 miles), Senegal (419-km, 260 miles) and Mauritania (2,237-km, 1390 miles).[14] These borders are difficult to control, facilitating untracked movement across the Sahel, the semi-arid zone between the Sahara Desert and the more arable lands in the south. The Sahel zone (also known as the trans-Sahel) is vast, approximately 1,000-km (621 miles) wide, and stretches across the continent from the Atlantic Ocean to the Red Sea. This transition zone is not true desert as areas of sparse seasonal vegetation, clay plains, and water holes can be found throughout the Sahel. Historically, pastoralists, such as the Tuareg ethnic group, migrated seasonally throughout this zone, maintaining a livelihood from camels, cattle, sheep, and goats, a practice long predating the creation of the current state boundaries.[15] In the era before long distance sea navigation, the trans-Saharan trade routes connected Africa to the Mediterranean zone and further on to Europe. Though foreboding and arduous, the Sahara has never been impassable, for thousands of years people, ideas, and goods have flowed across its sands.

Today, this vast, undergoverned space within the region has become a safe haven for Islamic militants, primarily AQIM and affiliated groups, as well as smugglers of weapons and drugs. The states in this region lack the resources, both financial and institutional capacity, to effectively meet the challenges of organized militancy and criminality. In many countries, this ungoverned space is in the hinterlands, physically and psychologically distant from the national capital. The capital cities of Nouakchott, located on the Atlantic Ocean, and Algiers and Tripoli on the Mediterranean Sea, are many hundreds of miles away from vast desert interiors of Mauritania, Algeria, and Libya, complicating efforts to exert effective control. Many of the countries in the region also face significant domestic political issues, and counterterrorism efforts must compete with other priorities, a fact that has complicated efforts to develop an effective regional security framework.

The potential for unrest in Mali to spread beyond its borders to vulnerable neighbors has raised international concern. In September 2012, António Guterres, the United Nations (UN) High Commissioner for Refugees and former prime minister of Portugal, warned that:

> If unchecked, the Mali crisis threatens to create an arc of instability extending west into Mauritania and east through Niger, Chad and Sudan to the Horn of Africa and the Gulf of Aden, characterized by extended spaces where state authority is weak and pockets of territorial control are exercised by transnational criminals.[16]

Within the international security community, the specter of collaboration among militant groups across this undergoverned territory is a growing concern:

> On the African continent, ties between radical groups Boko Haram, al Shabaab, al-Qaeda in the Islamic Maghreb (AQIM) and its offshoots—the Unity Movement for Jihad in West Africa (MUJAO) and Ansar Dine—are becoming stronger; as are ties with al-Qaeda in the Arabian Peninsula (AQAP) in Yemen.[17]

To use a Cold War analogy, one fear is that the collapse of Mali could unleash a domino effect—destabilizing countries throughout the Sahel for the benefit of criminals and militant groups, including AQIM. The freedom of movement found in an "arc of instability" that runs across the continent from the Atlantic coast of West Africa to the Horn of Africa on the Red Sea can be seen as a primary enabler for violent extremists in the region. Such freedom of movement could facilitate cooperation between groups such as AQIM, Ansar Dine, the Movement for Unity and Jihad in West Africa (MUJAO) in Mali, Boko Haram in Nigeria, and al Shabaab in Somalia. The recent discovery of instructions on how to avoid drone strikes in a building abandoned by AQIM in Mali, authored by Yemen-based al-Qaeda in the Arabian Peninsula (AQAP), illustrates the types of operational and technical cooperation across the network.[18] The document contained 22 tips, ranging from low technology approaches—attaching reflective pieces of glass to cars or the roofs of buildings—to the more sophisticated use of a Russian-made "sky grabber" device to infiltrate the drone's waves and the frequencies that can be purchased for around $2,595.[19]

Common to the countries through which this arc passes are "poverty, underdevelopment, illiteracy, mass youth unemployment, misgovernance, authoritarianism, corruption, suppression of women's rights as well as human and civil rights in general."[20] Many of these same characteristics could be found in the "Arab Spring" countries that experienced a wave of revolutions in 2011 suggesting they help create a fertile ground for revolution. While such mass popular movements may eventually lead to the development of a robust civil society and democratic institutions, the political and social disruption also create a window of opportunity for other actors, namely violent extremist organizations, to exercise control in the resulting security vacuum.

Finally, the humanitarian impact of the Malian crisis, addressed later in this monograph, is another reason this crisis matters. Described by General Carter F. Ham, the former commander of U.S. Africa Command (AFRICOM) as "patently the most difficult to address,"[21] the humanitarian condition is one of the spectrum of issues that must be addressed following the French intervention.

PART I - MALI: BACKGROUND TO A CRISIS

Mali: Ancient Grandeur, Modern Challenges.

A detailed exploration of Mali's history is well beyond the scope of this monograph, however, some aspects of Mali's historical development, as well as Mali's place in history provide essential context for understanding the dynamics that have led to the current crisis. Mali became an independent country only in 1960, its modern state identity is recent and often contested, with internal divisions and conditions that make it vulnerable to nonstate actors such as AQIM.

The origins of the modern state of Mali can be traced to the Malian Empire which existed from 1230 to 1600 CE. The Malian Empire began as a tribal confederation of the Mandika people united under Sunidiata Keita (c. 1217-55), who ruled under the name Mari Djata.[22] The empire consolidated and grew under his 25-year reign. The empire controlled a vast territory in West Africa that stretched to the Atlantic Ocean, a far larger area than that of the modern state.

Most of what the West knows of ancient Mali comes from the writings of Muslim scholars such as the Moroccan explorer Ibn Battuta (1304-68). Ibn Battuta left Sijilmasa, Morocco, on the northern edge of the Sahara and travelled south by caravan, stopping at oases and salt mines along the way. After 2 months, the caravan reached the southern junction of the trans-Saharan trade route, Oualata.[23] Ibn Battuta continued his journey on to Timbuktu, at the time a small provincial town; from there he went by canoe to Gao, an important center of trade.[24] Ibn Battuta's journey reflects the significance Mali had in the Islamic world at the time. His contemporary, the sociologist and historian Ibn Khaldun (1332-1406), recorded the royal genealogy of the Malian Empire, and captured some of the empire's oral history and traditions. Oral history was the norm by which events were embedded into the collective memory of the community.[25] Throughout West Africa, this oral history was preserved and passed down by *griots* (or *jeli*), a tradition that continues today. These oral historians held a prominent position in society, sometimes serving as advisors to the emperor.[26]

Gold was the main source of the empire's wealth, indeed it was gold and control over the trans-Saharan trade, that gave the Malian Empire its global significance. Gao and Timbuktu, on the edge of the Sahara, were vibrant trading centers and an economic crossroads into the desert and on to the Levant and Europe. Gold travelled north, salt travelled south. The empire enjoyed great periods of prosperity, especially under the famed ruler Mansa Musa.[27] Though the founder of the Malian Empire, Sundiata Keita (d. 1255) was not Muslim, the Mali Empire contained a diverse mix of ethnic groups and religions. The later adoption of Islam by Mali's rulers facilitated the spread of Islam into West Africa during the medieval period. A devout Muslim, Mansa Musa undertook the pilgrimage to Mecca in 1324, and historical accounts speak of a grand and lavish procession. He was accompanied by approximately 60,000 men. At that time, the Malian Empire controlled half of the world's supply of gold and salt. Eighty camels transported hundreds of pounds of gold dust, while 12,000 slaves each carried 4-pound bars of gold.[28] Musa spent so much gold in the bazaars of Cairo that gold prices were depressed and inflation rampant for a decade thereafter. The extravagance of this journey caught the attention of Western scholars and mapmakers, and knowledge of Timbuktu and Mali spread.

During the 15th century, Timbuktu grew into a center of Islamic scholarship and learning, in addition to trade. Mosques, libraries, and Koranic schools (madrasas) were constructed. By the 16th century, the city's population had grown to 100,000. The global cultural significance of Timbuktu's buildings, and the role of the city as a spiritual and intellectual center for the spread of Islam in Africa, was recognized in 1998 as a World Heritage Site by the United Nations Educational, Cultural and Scientific Organization (UNESCO). The site includes three earthen-brick mosques: Djingareyber, Sankore, and Sidi Yahia. Dating to the 13th century, they are considered exceptional examples of a building technique found typically in arid environments.[29] Sixteen mausoleums are also included on the list. Indeed, Timbuktu is also known as "the city of 333 saints," a reference to the many mausoleums of Sufi preachers and scholars constructed in the city over the centuries.[30]

Imperial Mali's leaders promoted Timbuktu's scholarly and intellectual development. Leo Africanus (1494-1554), the Moorish diplomat and historian, described the city in his geographical history of Africa:

There are in Timbuktu numerous judges, teachers and priests, all properly appointed by the king. He greatly honors learning. Many hand-written books imported from Barbary [North Africa] are also sold. There is more profit made from this commerce than from all other merchandise.[31]

So strong was the demand for learning that a distinct trans-Saharan book trade developed during the 12th and 13th centuries. Two types of books dominated the trade: (1) illuminated copies of the Koran, rich with calligraphy, and (2) less expensive, more functional copies of instructional and reference works.[32] The many mosques and schools in Timbuktu drove up demand for these texts. The University of Sankore (Masjid Sankore) alone contained 180 madrasas and 25,000 students.

Libraries, madrasas, scholars, and even families amassed collections of manuscripts. Before Islamic militants seized the city in 2012, Timbuktu was thought to contain as many as 300,000 antique manuscripts. Many of them were housed at the modern Ahmad Babu Institute, where they were restored and preserved; still others lay in private hands. The collection was priceless, containing manuscripts in Arabic as well as a few in African languages, "such as Songhai, Tamashek, and Bambara. There was even one in Hebrew. They covered a diverse range of topics including astronomy, poetry, music, medicine, and women's rights. The oldest dated from 1204."[33]

Timbuktu's cultural patrimony, its shared history of a multi-ethnic and multi-religious past, has come under severe attack, especially from the Tuareg Islamist militant group Ansar Dine. Ansar Dine began destroying the shrines in July 2012, taking pickaxes to them. Ansar Dine considers the Sufi shrines to be idolatrous and vowed to destroy all of them.[34] The Sidi Yahia mosque was also damaged. As they fled the city in January 2013, militant Islamists set fire to the Ahmad Babu Institute, and internationally funded library that restored, repaired, and stored irreplaceable manuscripts.[35] However, the loss is not nearly as great as first feared; quiet acts of resistance by Timbuktu's residents, who have long-cherished these manuscripts, saved many.

An imam (mosque leader) transferred 8,000 manuscripts to a secret location, many manuscripts are in the hands of private families — one hid their 3,000 item collection in another undisclosed location. At the Ahmad Babu Institute, nearly the entire collection was surreptitiously removed in small batches and sent to Bamako. Fleeing militants were able to find less than 5 percent of the collection.[36]

This is not the first time citizens of Timbuktu have hid their prized manuscripts from invaders, during the French colonial period, they hid them in wooden trunks, buried them in the sand, and secreted them in caves to keep them out of Europe's museums or private collections.[37] But in February 2013, it was French President François Hollande, alongside the Director General of UNESCO, who pledged to reconstruct and safeguard Timbuktu's cultural heritage.[38]

European Control of Africa.

The arrival of French forces into northern Mali in 2013 was, of course, a return to a country that France once controlled as part of a colonial empire, and that France continues to influence. Following centuries where Europe had relatively little contact with the continent, the 18th century saw a renewed interest, and a rediscovery of Africa on the part of Europe. With the invention of new navigational technology, such as the dry mariner's compass and marine astrolabe, European explorers no longer hugged the African coastline, but ventured out across the oceans, launching the "Age of Exploration."[39] Europe had turned toward the New World and its riches. The global economic world system was dramatically altered, land routes that controlled trade for centuries were surpassed by sea routes, and major trade cities such as Cairo went into decline, while other cities captured the new global trade driven by Europe.[40]

Exploration of the continent and its interior in the 18th century and competition between rival European imperial powers drove European interest in Africa. In 1798, Napoleon Bonaparte launched a military campaign in Syria and Egypt. While the stated goal was to protect French trade interests, the French intent was to limit Britain's access to the "jewel" of its overseas empire, India. The Napoleonic campaign was no ordinary military engagement. Nearly 200 scientists participated in a scientific expedition; its goal was to catalog the artifacts of ancient and modern Egypt as well as its natural history. The result was published in a series of large volumes, entitled the *Description de l'Égypte*, which helped feed a growing European appetite for the "orient."[41]

The exploits of explorers such as Sir Richard Burton further fueled interest. Often sponsored by the British Royal Geographic Society, Burton carried out a series of daring explorations in the mid-century. He became well known after making the Islamic pilgrimage (hajj) to Mecca, and then turned to exploration of Africa's interior, in search of the origin of the Nile River. Burton was a very prolific writer, writing hundreds of books and articles on his various adventures.[42] At the same time, David Livingstone explored south and central Africa and named the renowned waterfall "Victoria Falls" in honor of the Queen of England. All European contact with Livingstone was lost for 6 years and his death was rumored, a tale that gripped the public. This fascination with Africa, and geopolitical rivalry, was not limited to Europe. In 1869 the anti-British editor of the *New York Herald* ordered his journalist, Henry Morton Stanley, to find and rescue the lost explorer. His successful search led to the — possibly apocryphal — account of their meeting: "Dr. Livingstone, I presume?"[43]

Europe was now convinced of Africa's strategic importance, a result of both location and the numerous accounts of the continent's vast untapped resources. For Europe's voracious imperial appetite, Africa was the last frontier that could be exploited. In 1884-85, a conference was held in Berlin, Germany, to set the ground rules among the European powers for colonization and trade activities. In reality, the "Congo Conference" formalized the rules for the rapid expansion of European interests in Africa, also known as the "Scramble for Africa." The conference participants accepted the concept of "effective occupation" in determining which country could claim a geographical area. Means of establishing effective occupation included entering into treaties with local, indigenous leaders, establishing an administrative presence and maintaining order with a police force.[44] As soon as the ground rules were laid down, European countries raced against each other to claim a territory as their own.

Mali Under French Control.

The area that encompasses Mali today was originally part of a French colonial territory known as the French Sudan formed in 1890.[45] Though there were rumors of the region's great wealth, no doubt a legacy of the medieval accounts, France's primary interest in the area was to link their holdings in Senegal and Algeria and provide access to the Congo and its riches through Lake Chad. France had seized Algeria against great opposition in 1830. Algeria was a central component of France's overseas empire; it was integrated into metropolitan France as a department in 1848 and became part of French political life. France's economic ties with Algeria were deep, and tens of thousands of Europeans settled there.

European states, especially France, Netherlands, and Portugal, had long competed for trade along the Senegalese coastline. In 1444, Portugal established a major center for slave trading on the Island of Goreé; Britain seized control of it as a result of the Napoleonic Wars (1803-15) and abolished slavery. France's involvement in West Africa began in 1637, when they built a fort at the mouth of the Senegal River and began to explore the interior. By the 1850s, France was working to establish control further inland in order to consolidate its colonial empire.[46]

The French Sudan was part of a set of colonies that made up the Federation of West Africa (existed from 1865 to 1960), which included Senegal, French Guinea, Cote d'Ivoire, Upper Volta (Burkina Faso), Niger, Mauritania, and Dahomey (Benin today). French West Africa encompassed an area of approximately 1.8 million square miles (4,689,000 square kilometers [km]) and a diverse population composed of a great many ethnic groups who spoke many languages. Within the federation, French was the common language. France also established a common currency, the French West African Franc.[47] Each colony of French West Africa was administered by a Lieutenant Governor, responsible to the Governor General in Dakar, Senegal. Only the Governor General received orders from Paris. France also held colonies in adjacent North Africa, as well as a few in equatorial Africa and East Africa, and numerous island possessions.

The Pacification of the Sahel.

French penetration and control of the interior of the French Sudan was met with significant resistance. There was little French presence in the interior prior to the 1850s. French explorer René Callié was the first European to visit Timbuktu (1827) and return alive; a British officer, Major Gordon Laign, had preceded his arrival in the city but was killed shortly after he departed. Callié published his account of his journey in *Journal d'un voyage à Temboctou et à Jenné dans l'Afrique Centrale*.[48]

Callié was eager to reach Timbuktu, which he described as "an object of curiosity and research to the civilised nations of Europe." What he found, however, was a disappointment:

> I looked around and found that the sight before me, did not answer my expectations. I had formed a totally different idea of the grandeur and wealth of Timbuctoo. The city presented, at first view, nothing but a mass of ill-looking houses, built of earth.[49]

Indeed, in the centuries since historians had recorded accounts of the Mali Empire at its height, much had changed. By the mid-1600s, the empire had broken up into three parts, following a succession dispute. This left the empire vulnerable to attack by others, namely the Bamana people of nearby Djenne. The Timbuktu Callié found was greatly diminished from that described during the reign of strong emperors such as Mansa Musa. The social and political fragmentation that characterized the 19th century western Sahel both aided and hindered French expansion. While the French did not have to overcome a strong and well-organized empire, the fragmentation meant dealing with a great many, often competing, ethnic groups and even kinship groups in an effort to establish control. Local inhabitants offered much resistance; there was no real effective French control until 1899.

European colonialism was based on the desire to bring "Christianity, civilization, and commerce" to Africa. Callié's account of the death of Major Laing reinforced the justification for European colonialism. According to Callié's published account, Major Laing was killed after refusing to convert to Islam:

> When the major had once been discovered to be a Christian and a European, death was a thousand times preferable to even a temporary change of religion, since he must have renounced all hope of again visiting Europe.[50]

Callié described many of the ethnic groups he encountered during his journey such as the Moors and Fulani. The Tuaregs (Tooariks), who he calls "mauraders" and "savages" receive the most negative description. Remarking on their control of the desert, he notes that "The trade of Timbuctoo is considerably cramped by the Tooariks, a warlike nation who render the inhabitants of the town their tributaries."[51] This negative image of the Tuareg was further reinforced in later encounters with the French military as they tried to "pacify" the Sahel and improve the value of their colonies through construction of roads and railroads.

In 1880-81, an expedition led by French Colonel Paul Flatters set out to survey a route for a railroad that would cross the Sahara. Composed of 300 camels, 10 French soldiers, and 78 "native" guides and porters, the expedition sought to cross the territory controlled by one of the tribes that made up the confederation of Tuaregs in the Sahel. The leader of the Tuaregs denied them permission to cross his territory; likely realizing construction of a railroad would mean an end to his economic livelihood, the caravan trade. Colonel Flatters continued into the territory and found himself drawn into an ambush. Lack of food and water led to further casualties. None of the French survived, causing a furor in France with demands that the Tuaregs be punished. However, it would be another 17 years before the French attempted to establish control again.[52]

In 1899, France launched three military missions from Senegal, Algeria, and the Congo to consolidate their holdings and to bring them under French control. The Voulet-Chanoine Mission, which set out from Dakar, Senegal, ended in scandal following the death of the commanding officers at the hands of their own soldiers.

Captain Paul Voulet and Adjutant Lieutenant Julien Chanoine led the mission; the other Europeans included nine officers, a doctor, and three noncommissioned officers. The mission was accompanied by approximately 100 guides and interpreters, as well as over 1,000 porters and others that were conscripted to support the heavily armed mission. Their goal was to

19

move through the French Sudan, the interior still had not submitted to French rule, and reach Lake Chad. The mission carried few supplies; they were expected to live off the land:

> To get the porters and food they needed, Voulet and Chanoine burned villages, enslaved populations and massacred those they did not need. By the time they were stopped by another French column, their ranks had swollen to about 3,000, mostly slave women. Historians have often treated Voulet and Chanoine as men who went mad in the tropical sun, but Fuglestad argues that the atrocities were simply an extravagant version of what the French military did elsewhere.[53]

When French authorities learned of the atrocities being committed, they sent a column of troops led by Lieutenant Colonel Jean-François Klobb to relieve Voulet of his command. Voulet killed Klobb, further heightening the scandal. The Voulet-Chanoine affair, the high cost of maintaining the military presence in the French Sudan, and internal French political turmoil, including the Dreyfus Affair, all led to a reassessment of the military-led pacification strategy for the Sudan. Control over the Sudan was shifted to the civilian colonial government, and military operations were restricted.[54] Resistance to French control in the Sahara continued well into the 1930s, when airplanes allowed greater ability to track the Sahel's population.[55]

Even outside the areas that faced military pacification, colonial policies affected the indigenous African population. To improve the colony, Africans were forced to work without pay on public works such as road building. They could be imprisoned without trial and could not engage in political activity. They were subject to military draft.[56] Indeed, thousands of African soldiers fought and died in World Wars I and II, where they played a pivotal role in the liberation of France from Nazi Germany:

> On Aug. 15, 1944, two months after the Allied landings in Normandy, a French force of 200,000, with an estimated 65 percent of them from former colonies, landed in Provence with the U.S. Seventh Army. They fought through the suburbs of Toulon and Marseille, moving on to help repel the Germans from the eastern Vosges Mountains and Alsace before crossing the Rhine. Historians estimate that about 40,000 troops of African origin died liberating the country.[57]

When French troops entered in Mali's northern cities in 2013, some Malians held signs recalling the role of Mali in liberating France.

Malian Independence.

The movement toward decolonization in Africa grew very quickly after World War II. Many African countries experienced a growing wave of nationalism and a desire for independence. For the European imperial states, their economies shattered by war, far flung overseas colonies were expensive to keep. Intensifying violent nationalist movements among the colonial subjects made the price even steeper. In Kenya, for example, the Mau Mau Rebellion against British control broke out in 1952. Shortly thereafter, France found themselves engaged in an increasingly bloody guerrilla war in Algeria.[58]

The Algerian War for Independence (or Algerian Revolution) lasted from 1954 to 1962. It was extremely costly, both financially and in loss of life. The war was characterized by the use of insurgent tactics in an urban environment, famously depicted in the film, *The Battle of Algiers*. By 1956, over 400,000 French troops were committed to Algeria.[59] Backlash over the handling of the Algerian war led to fall of the French Fourth Republic and the return of General Charles de Gaulle to power. In 1959, he declared that "self-determination" would be the preferred solution to the Algerian conflict.[60] Following referendums in France and Algeria as well as long negotiations, Algerian independence was granted on July 3, 1962. Death tolls for the conflict range from 400,000 to 1.5 million.[61]

The French Sudan received independence from France in 1960, in the midst of the crisis over Algeria. In the post-World War II period, relations between France and its territories in West Africa were marked by debate over the nature of the relationship between France and the colonies. Among the African elite, who had assimilated much of French culture and on whom the French depended to administer the colonies, slogans such as "federalism" and "independence" took center stage. At the same time, the French authorities began to allow indigenous political activity and the formation of political parties. Britain's announcement that the Gold Coast (present day Ghana) would become independent in 1957 further drove the movement toward independence in French Sudan. French control over West Africa was dealt a steep blow in 1958 when Guinea voted "no" on a referendum to continue an association with France, and relations between the two countries were cut. Shortly thereafter, the Sudanese Republic (Mali) and Senegal joined a federation, while other colonies sought independent statehood. Together, they achieved independence in 1960 as the Mali Federation.[62] Their union did not last, and, after a few months, Senegal withdrew, and the Sudanese Republic was renamed Mali.[63]

PART II: THE CRISIS UNFOLDS

Mali: The Challenges of Development.

Like other newly independent countries in Africa, Mali faced enormous political, geographic, and economic challenges at independence, and many of these persist into the present, contributing to the underlying causes of the current crisis. Unsurprisingly, state level institutions for governance and politics were underdeveloped or absent in the newly independent state. According to William Foltz, specific issues Mali faced included:

> Separation of the political process and governmental activity from the lives of most people . . . Existence of a small, relatively homogeneous political elite, lack of stable internal political process permitting a peaceful and democratic replacement of elites and offering the possibility of a return to political office once a person has lost a political contest.[64]

Mali's first president, the nationalist leader Modibo Keita, was elected to the presidency of the Mali Federation in 1960; when the federation dissolved, he became president of Mali, a position he held until 1968. In 1968, General Moussa Traoré overthrew Keita in a coup d'état. Under Traoré's 2 decades of rule, Mali was a virtual police state in which political activity was not tolerated. The repressive climate eventually brought an end to Traoré's 23-year regime. Robert Pringle, who served as U.S. ambassador to Mali between 1987 and 1990 observed:

In March 1991, Mali's military dictator made the fatal mistake of ordering his troops to fire on students protesting in the capital, and several hundred were killed. In the wave of shocked public reaction that followed, a key military commander, Colonel Amadou Toumani Touré, joined the pro-democracy forces, and the dictatorship collapsed. Touré, better known as "ATT," promised to hand over power to an elected government. Like Cincinnatus, the Roman farmer who took up arms and then returned to his fields, Touré kept his word, surprising many of his fellow Malians.[65]

Touré's decision to relinquish power to the civilian government launched a new political era in Mali, characterized by democratic processes rather than violent overthrow:

Until the 1992 presidential election Malians had never experienced a change of government by means other than a coup d'état. A decade later the 2002 election of ATT to the presidency marked the first time in Mali's history that power would be passed from one democratically elected president to another.[66]

This success made Mali a symbol of Africa's democratic potential. After the 1992 elections, Mali held successful, multiparty presidential elections again in 1997, reelecting President Alpha Oumar Konaré to a second 5-year term.[67] In 2002, a field of 24 candidates vied for the presidency. After two rounds of voting, Touré returned to power, transformed from a military to a civilian leader. He was elected to a second term in 2007. Mali was seen not only as an "African" success story for democracy but also offered proof that Islam and democracy were compatible.

> While radical Islam has inhibited the creation of democratic institutions in other parts of the Muslim world, Malians do not widely perceive such radicalism as a threat to their democracy. Indeed, radical Islam seems to be growing slowly — if at all — in Mali. Further, Malians see the long-standing problem of unrest and near anarchy in the desert north not as a democratization problem but rather as a security problem — that is, as a threat to national unity.[68]

Eventually, this conflict in the north, fueled in part by radical Islamists, felled Malian democracy when Touré's civilian government was overthrown in a coup led by Captain Amadou Sanago in March 2012. President Touré went into hiding after the coup, but in April he resigned as part of a deal negotiated with the coup leaders by the ECOWAS. Under the deal, parliamentary leader Dioncounda Traoré, was sworn in as interim president at the head of a transitional administration pending new presidential elections set for July 2013.[69] Touré is now in exile in Senegal.

Mali, like many young states in Africa, has a weak sense of national unity and national identity. Geography poses significant challenge's to Mali's economic and political development and undermines national unity. Mali has no outlet to the sea, but West Africa's largest river, the Niger, which originates in the highland of Guinea, flows through it. The river passes through many of the country's important cities, such as Bamako, Timbuktu, and Gao, before entering the ocean along the coast of Niger. Mali is composed of three distinct regions, delineated primarily by the amount of rainfall, which ranges from 0 millimeters (mm) of annual precipitation in the north to 1,550-mm in the extreme south. The Sudanese climate of the south allows considerable agricultural production, while grasslands are common in the semi-arid Sahel zone. In the north, the Saharan Desert dominates the countryside.[70] Economic opportunities, lifestyle, and population characteristics differ dramatically across these zones. Political and economic power is strongly centered on the urban elites in south of the country.

Mali's population is very diverse, containing many ethnic groups. The Manding (Mandé) peoples account for half of Mali's population and include the Bambara and Malinka ethnic groups. These two groups, which live in southern Mali near the capital of Bamako, are the largest and most politically dominant. They tend to make up the elite that benefited from French education during the colonial period.

The Peulh (also called Fula or Fulani) account for about 11 percent of the population, and they farm or herd cattle in the Niger delta. The Seina (also called Senoufo), make up 9.6 percent of the population. They are primarily farmers, though many have migrated to cities for work, and live in south-east Mali.

The Soninké who live in north-west Mali's Sahelian zone make up 7 percent of Mali's population. They trace their roots to the Ghana Empire, and trade is a very important part of their economic life. The Songhai are descendants of the people of the Soghai Empire that once existed around Gao. They compose 7 percent of Mali's population and engage in subsistence farming in southeastern Mali.

The Tuareg and the Maure (Moor) make up about 5 percent of the population. Located in northern Mali, the Maure are Arab-Berbers that migrate with their herds between Mali and Mauritiania. The Tuareg, or Kel Tamasheq (Tamasheq-speaking people) as they refer to themselves, are nomadic pastoralists, ethnically related to Berbers, who are among the indigenous inhabitants of the Sahel and Saharan region. Countries with significant Tuareg populations include Niger (1.7 million), Mali (1.4 million), Algeria (825,000), Libya (620,000), and Burkina Faso (330,000).[71] The Tuareg are primarily Muslim, though they practice a syncretic form of Islam, which blends many forms of pre-Islamic and indigenous practices.[72] In Mali, they are predominately located in the north of the country, including the main population centers of Gao, Kidal, and Timbuktu. The Tuaregs are also notable for the blue, indigo-dyed "veils" worn by males to protect them from the desert sands while riding. Though the Tuareg are Muslim, women traditionally do not wear the veil.

Despite the diversity of Malian society, inter-ethnic and inter-religious tolerance has been the norm.[73] This is, in part, attributed to the presence of syncretic forms of Islam that blend Islam, including Sufi variations, with traditional practices and beliefs. Until the involvement of radical Islamist groups in the Tuareg rebellion in the north, political and economic marginalization, not religious beliefs and ethnicity, were the foci of the conflict. Today, however, there are new ethnic and religious dimensions to the crisis.

Other minority groups include the Dogon (4 percent of population), Bozo (2.8 percent), Diawara (1 percent), and Xaasongaxango (1 percent). Mali is predominantly Muslim (90 percent), with a small number of Christians (4 percent) as well as others who follow traditional religions. French is the official language, Bambara is widely spoken. Other widely-spoken languages include Fulfulde (Peulh), Songhai, and Tamasheq, however, a great many other languages exist.[74]

Approximately 90 percent of Mali's 16.3 million people live in the south, with the remainder distributed across the country's sparsely inhabited north, which inhibits effective integration of these areas, and their peoples, into the state. Most of the state's resources are focused on the south and its population. The north, particularly the Kidal administrative region inhabited by the Tuaregs, is very poor in comparison with the rest of the country, with little local economic activity. The region depends highly on foreign aid, which is focused on projects such as road building, irrigation, health, and education.[75]

Mali scores very low by most development measures. Ranked 182 out of 187 on the United Nations Human Development Index (HDI), Mali is labeled a "low human development" country. The HDI is a composite measure that compares life expectancy, literacy, education, standards of living, and quality of life. Mali's average life expectancy is 51.9 years, and adults attend only 2 years of school on average.[76]

Economically, under the World Bank classification system, Mali is considered a low-income country. The gross national income per capita (GNI) in 2011 was $610. Poverty levels are high, and 43.6 percent live below the national poverty line.[77] Mali's economy is highly undiversified, and the country is dealing with one of the highest population growth rates in the world. In 2011, the population growth rate was 3 percent, driven by a total fertility rate of 6.2 percent.[78] Mali must also deal with the effects of climate change.[79]

The northern Sahel zone is particularly hard hit by the consequences of climate change. Drought and desertification have increased the population's vulnerability and raised levels of food insecurity. Mali's average annual rainfall has decreased 30 percent since

1998; droughts are longer and more common. Desertification, where land is becoming increasingly arid, is also a problem in Mali where the Sahara is moving southward at a rate of 48-km, about 30 miles, a year.[80] As a result of the Sahara's southern movement, Mali is experiencing "climate zone shift." This shift will bring additional negative consequences to Mali. According to 22 global climate models that forecast to 2030, the most negative scenario could mean a decrease in rainfall by 10 percent and an increase in average temperatures by 1.8 degrees fahrenheit (1.4 degrees celsius). This scenario would result in a $300 million agricultural loss for Mali. Even under the most optimistic climate models, annuals losses of $120 million are forecast.[81] This anticipated climate change will put even greater strains on the population and society in northern Mali, and increase the potential for instability that can be exploited by criminals and militants.

Early Indicators of a Crisis in Northern Mali.

The building crisis in northern Mali went unnoticed by most people in the West. In hindsight, there were numerous, though perhaps unconventional, indicators of increasing instability. Essakane, an oasis settlement located 50 miles west of Timbuktu, is well-known to world music fans. Long a trading location for the Tuareg, it is home to a deep musical tradition, whose sounds evoke comparison with American blues music.

Since 2001, Essakane had hosted the "Festival au Desert," drawing international stars, such as Robert Plant, musicians from throughout Africa, and thousands of Western spectators every year. Just a few short years ago, a journalist described this scene:

In a normal December, the streets of Timbuktu are crawling with Western tourists. They take tours of the local libraries full of 12th-century manuscripts, ride camels into the desert to spend the night under the stars, and in early January, attend the Festival au Desert, a kind of Saharan Woodstock, where Tuareg and Malian guitarists trade blues riffs.[82]

By 2010, in response to the rising number of kidnappings of Westerners in the region by AQIM, the Malian authorities moved the festival closer in, to the outskirts of Timbuktu. In November 2011, three European tourists were kidnapped and a German tourist killed in Timbuktu.[83] These attacks, the first in the city itself, clearly sought to undermine the tourism industry. The attacks, part of a increasingly bold strategy of kidnappings used by AQIM since 2008, brought additional security to the 2012 Festival au Desert.

In 2013, the organizers announced the festival would be moved south to Burkina Faso. Not only had the festival site been destroyed, but speaking from the city of Gao in August 2012, a spokesman for the MUJAO, a splinter group of AQIM, issued a ban on all Western music. In their press release, the organizers noted, "It is an attack on our collective memory, on all that unites the many ethnic groups of Timbuktu."[84]

In northern Mali, AQIM applied a classic al-Qaeda strategy to gain control of territory from which they could operate. AQIM capitalized on the lack of effective Malian central government presence in the region, while leveraging the existing conflict between the Tuareg and the central government to their benefit. External factors, such as the Arab Spring and fall of Gadaffi's regime, also worked to AQIM's advantage, as it helped drive a new phase of the Tuareg rebellion and contributed to the conditions that led to the military coup. Though the United States and its partners had created a regional security framework to meet the threat posed by al-Qaeda, this framework was fragile, contained many weaknesses, and could not withstand the set of events that led to AQIM's control over the country's north.

The Tuareg Rebellions.

An ethnic minority, geographically remote from Mali's capital, the Tuareg have long felt politically and economically marginalized. During both the French colonial period and after Malian independence, the integration of the highly independent Tuaregs into the state has been a much contested issue. The Tuaregs have a long history of conflict with the central government. Historically, these conflicts, which tend to center on the administrative region of Kidal, have been motivated by politics and economics, not religious extremism:

> The most important single element in recent northern unrest has been political disaffection among one group of Tuareg inhabiting the region around Kidal, northeast of Timbuktu. This disaffection is well documented and has had little to do with religion; rather, it has been a classic case of conflict between nomads and central authority.[85]

Tuareg aspirations traditionally focus on independence or autonomy, not the creation of a religious state or caliphate. As a result, the Tuareg separatist movement, led by the National Movement for the Liberation of Azawad (MNLA), raises a potential challenge to Mali's territorial integrity and internal stability. From the Malian central government perspective, the Tuareg actions are a rebellion or insurgency.

The idea of a Tuareg homeland, Azawad, comprised of Tuareg populated areas in northern Mali, northern Niger, and southern Algeria came into being in the 1950s. In Mali, Azawad would include the provinces of Gao, Kidal, and Timbuktu in the north; constituting about half of Mali's total territory. The French briefly considered the idea of creating an independent state for the Tuareg, which met with great resistance by Mali and other countries with a Tuareg population. Also at that time, the Tuareg's identity and loyalty was primarily focused on their local communities, not nationalist aspirations.[86] Indeed, even today, it is not clear how much of the Tuareg community supports an independent state, and political identity remains highly localized.

The current Tuareg rebellion in Mali, which started January 17, 2012, is the fourth wave in a long-standing series of conflicts between some members of the Tuareg population and the Malian government. The first rebellion occurred in 1963, and involved the Kidal Tuareg who resented the government's attempts to reduce their autonomy.[87] The Tuareg attacked government targets in quick raids. Armed with Soviet weaponry, the Malian army conducted a vigorous counterinsurgency campaign and easily defeated the Tuaregs, who were equipped with camels and outdated small arms. The rebellion was crushed by 1964, and the northern Tuareg areas placed under repressive military administration. During the conflict, many of Mali's Tuaregs fled into neighboring countries. Lieutenant Colonel Kalifa Keita of the Malian Army noted:

While the government had succeeded in ending the rebellion, its coercive measures alienated many Tuaregs who had not supported the insurgents. Atrocities and human rights abuses on both sides contributed to a climate of fear and distrust in the north. And while the government subsequently announced a number of programs to improve local infrastructure and economic opportunity, it lacked the resources to follow through on most of them. As a result, Tuareg grievances remained largely unaddressed, and a seething resentment continued in many Tuareg communities after 1964. Clearly the problem of instability had been deferred, not resolved.[88]

The tactics used by the Malian military included "massacres, poisoning of wells, and destruction of flocks," all actions that violate Muslim principles of warfare. Indeed, the governmental response to the 1963 rebellion still resonates in Tuareg popular culture. In 2012, the Tuareg desert blues band, Tinariwen, recorded the song, *Soixante-Trois* (63):

'63 has gone, but will return.
Those days have left their traces.
They murdered the old folk and a child just born.
They swooped down to the pastures and wiped out the cattle . . .
'63 has gone, but will return.[89]

The Malian counterinsurgency campaign created a long-standing bitterness that would be fueled by growing perceptions of economic and political marginalization.

Periods of devastating drought in the Sahel between 1968 and 1974 and again from 1980 to 1985 destroyed much of the region's livestock. Without these economic assets, many Tuaregs became refugees in neighboring countries or were forced to work as day laborers in southern Mali to survive. The loss of their traditional livelihoods deeply undermined the fabric of Tuareg society and added to social instability.[90] In the late-1980s, large numbers of Tuaregs who had been working in Libya lost their jobs after the collapse of world oil prices. Gaddafi had courted the Tuareg, using radio broadcasts to urge them to join his military. When Libya's attempt to militarily annex Chad in 1986 failed, many of these Tuaregs, who had served as front line troops while Libyans were more protected in the rear, returned to Mali.[91] These events, in addition to the long-standing and unresolved grievance from the 1963 rebellion, fueled a second rebellion in 1990.

The 1990 rebellion was led by the Popular Movement for the Liberation of Azawad (MPLA: *Mouvement Populaire de Libération de l'Azawad*), formed by Tuareg exiles living in Algeria, including Iyad ag Ghali.[92] The 1990 rebellion began with a MPLA attack conducted on a police post by a small group of Tuareg soldiers recently returned from Libyan army camps killing 18.[93] The Traoré government, under increasing pressure to allow more political participation, used the rebellion as an excuse to cancel multiparty elections. He fueled tensions between the north and south of the country by "portraying the Tuareg as 'white-dominated feudal society' that relied on black slavery to preserve their traditional way of life."[94]

An Algerian-brokered peace treaty, signed April 11, 1992, between the Unified Movements and Fronts of Azawad and the Malian government (really a transitional government following a military coup that ended Moussa Traoré's 23-year rule in April 1991) ended the second rebellion. Known as the Tamanrasset Accord for the city in Algeria where it was signed, it contained provisions for a cease-fire, subsequent integration of former combatants into special units of Malian armed forces, a repatriation program for people displaced by the conflict, and acknowledgement of the special status of Northern Mali.[95] Northern Mali was to have increased autonomy and greater control over its own governance.

One of the most significant results of the Tamanrasset Accord was the formation of temporary security forces to garrison the north. These forces contained a fixed percentage of Malian Army and rebel combatants. The program was both a confidence building measure, as well as an employment generating mechanism directed at unemployed, armed Tuareg youths. By early 1998, "some 3000 Tuaregs combatants — probably more than ever were in the field as rebels at any one time — have been integrated into the various Malian security forces and civil service."[96] However, from the Tuareg perspective, many of the main components of the Tamanrasset Accord were never honored.[97] Also, the decision to sign an agreement with the government of Mali was not unanimous within the MPLA, the agreement encouraged splintering within the group. As a result, though the MPLA formally disbanded in 1996, other groups, sometimes including members from the former MPLA, formed, and resentment continued to simmer.

In May 2006, violence again erupted; this so-called third rebellion lasted until 2009 and was focused primarily in the Kidal region. The perception of discrimination was again at the core of Tuareg complaints. A newly formed group, The May 23 Democratic Alliance for Change (ADC, *Alliance Democratique du 23 mai pour le Changement*) was active in this rebellion.[98]

Included in the movement was Ibrahim Ag Bahanga, a former MPLA member and former rebel who had been integrated into the Malian armed forces under the Tamanrasset Accord. The complaints of the soldiers centered on the slow pace of promotion through the military ranks and the nature of their assignments. As in previous rebellions, attacks focused on government targets, including the military garrisons at Kidal and Menaka.[99] Algeria again helped to broker an agreement between the government of Mali led by President Touré and the Tuareg. The Algiers Accords (July 2006) included greater autonomy for the Kidal region, economic development measures, and a larger role for local Tuareg in security forces. Despite the accord, conflict continued as a new faction of the ADC emerged led by Ibrahim Ag Bahanga. The ADC continued attacks, taking 23 Malian soldiers hostage in August 2007. These attacks were denounced by the former leadership of the ADC, including Iyad Ag Ghali who had since run for office and was integrated into politics.

The most recent Tuareg rebellion took place in October 2011. As Gaddafi's regime crumbled, leaders of the various Tuareg factions met and formed the MNLA. Its membership drew former soldiers from Gaddafi's army, including its leader, Colonel Ag Mohamed Najem, and deserters from the Malian military.[100] The October meeting at a desert oasis was an attempt to ward off the splintering that had long undermined the Tuareg armed movements. An MNLA statement released at the time declared, "We've overcome our differences and will now present common political demands which reflect the profound aspirations of our population." Demands included immediate negotiations with the Malian government.[101] The most recent outbreak of the rebellion in January 2012 followed failed attempts at dialog between the Malian government and the MNLA.[102]

On January 17, 2012, MNLA forces attacked and captured the northern town of Menaka, near the border with Niger. In the weeks that followed, Tuareg rebels established control over much of northern Mali, including Gao, which contains the largest military base in northern Mali and a strategically significant military base at Tessalit. Shortly after the March 21 coup in which members of the Malian military overthrew the government of President Touré, the MNLA established control over Timbuktu.[103] Outrage by some members of the Mali military over the government's failure to properly equip troops to fight the heavily armed Tuareg force was a factor in the coup led by Captain Amadou Sanogo.[104] The coup members accused President Touré of "incompetence in the fight against Islamic terror."[105] The coup, and the subsequent collapse of Mali's military presence in the north, benefitted the MNLA and enabled consolidation of their gains. However, the secular MNLA eventually found itself pushed aside by AQIM and its affiliate, Ansar Dine.

The Impact of the Libyan Revolution.

Though many of the underlying causes of Mali's complex security challenge have existed for decades, the overthrow of Gaddafi's regime and the return of heavily armed Tuareg fighters from Libya upset the precarious balance of power in northern Mali.[106] The wave of change, often referred to as the Arab Spring, which swept through North Africa also reenergized the Tuareg's long-standing quest for greater autonomy, or perhaps independence, in a geographic area that includes much of northern Mali.

Libyan leader Muammar Gaddafi had long employed Tuaregs in his military, utilizing them in conflicts both in Libya and Chad, and further afield in Afghanistan and Lebanon. In 1980, he declared Libya the natural homeland of all Tuaregs and offered them Libyan nationality.[107] When Gaddafi lost power in October 2011, an estimated 2,000 to 4,000 Malian Tuareg fighters returned home.[108] These fighters were heavily armed; the looting and sale of weapons from the Libyan government's arsenal created a sudden influx of heavy weaponry in the region.[109] Of specific concern were the 20,000 man operated portable air defense systems (MANPAD) the Libyan government had in its arsenal prior to the revolution. Of these, 5,000 have been secured by a multinational team under implementation of a UN disarmament, demobilization, and reintegration program. An unknown number are thought to have been destroyed during conflict, but fears remain that some of the weapons have been transported outside of Libya and may be in the hands of armed groups.[110] The operational condition of these weapons is not known, as weaponry were often poorly maintained by Gaddafi's forces, but operational MANPADs pose a significant threat to aircraft.

The MLNA claimed to have 1,000 well-armed fighters;[111] while government forces, prior to the 2012 coup, were estimated at 7,350.[112] The level of military experience and weaponry possessed by the current rebels may distinguish it from previous, less well-armed and organized rebellions. The MNLA leaders, Ag Mohamed Najem and Bilal Ag Acherif, held the rank of colonel in Gaddafi's army. Also, other members obtained significant military experience in earlier

rebellions and the Libyan civil war.[113] Some high rank-
ing officers from the Malian army, such as Lieutenant
Colonel Ag Mbarek Kay and Colonel Ag Bamoussa,
also bring significant experience to the group.[114] The
MNLA had assembled an impressive arsenal, accu-
mulated over a number of years of planning and forti-
fied by heavy weaponry brought by fighters returned
from Libya. They also had experience implementing
long-range guerrilla tactics over distances of hundreds
of miles.[115]

AQIM in North Africa.

There is no doubt that the Tuareg rebellion, coup,
and the end of Gaddafi's regime created new opportunities for AQIM to expand its influence in the Sahel and West Africa. AQIM traces its roots to Algeria. Formerly known as the Salafist for Preaching and
Combat group (GSPC, *Salafist pour la Predication et le
Combat*), they are a splinter group from the Armed
Islamic Group (GIA) that fought a civil war against
Algeria's secular government in the late-1990s. They
aligned themselves with al-Qaeda in the early 2000s,
and changed their name to AQIM in 2006 after their
pledge of loyalty was accepted by the al-Qaeda leadership.[116] However, the extent that AQIM is controlled
or influenced by the al-Qaeda leadership in Afghanistan and Pakistan is not clear.[117]

Successful Algerian counterterrorism measures
drove AQIM from Algiers and the surrounding area,
pushing them deeper into southern Algeria and
neighboring countries. AQIM's increasing presence in
the Sahel is marked by a campaign of kidnappings for
ransom and attempted kidnappings, focused on both
tourists as well as UN and U.S. diplomats and aid

workers, the killing of a number of hostages and an assassination of a Malian military official.[118] Kidnapping for ransom has proven to be very lucrative for AQIM; between 2006 and 2011, they are believed to have received an estimated $70 million.[119] Their overall strategy, according to Modibo Goita, is to create sanctuaries in which to operate, as part of the "Afghanization of the entire Sahel region."[120]

Common al-Qaeda themes and narratives characterize AQIM's messaging:

> The bulk of AQIM's messages, the speeches and statements, consist of the broad strands of Salafi-jihadi rhetoric, with frequent references to fitna (disorder), jahiliyya (pre-Islamic ignorance), fasad (corruption), and the importance of fighting for the return of the proper way of life. Like other countries al-Qaeda has targeted, AQIM argues that the governments of Algeria, Libya, Mali, Mauritania, Morocco, and Tunisia are composed of unbelievers and need to be replaced by governments that adhere to a strict interpretation of Islamic law (Shari'a).[121]

An additional goal is to rid the region of foreign influences, namely the United States and France. In mid-2010, following the death of a French hostage and AQIM calls for attacks on France, French government officials rebutted, saying that they were "at war with al-Qaeda."[122]

The extent of the relationship and cooperation between AQIM and various factions of Tuareg rebels is a matter of debate; it is clear that the security vacuum benefited them both.

However, the MNLA had been very adamant about its relationship to AQIM, denying in strong terms any possible link to al-Qaeda,[123] and claimed it would stand as a buffer against it.[124] Though not ideologically aligned, there are shared interests, and perhaps a pragmatic alliance, between AQIM and members of the Tuaregs, including tribal ties and smuggling of an array of items including cigarettes, migrants, and weapons.[125] Such illegal activities are even more important today in a region that has seen its primary form of legitimate economic activity, tourism, disappear amid AQIM violence, raising the prospect that people may turn to AQIM, or at least tolerate them, for economic reasons. "Misery has made the Sahel's thousands of unemployed an easy target for recruiters from extremist groups."[126]

AQIM has pursued an integration strategy in Mali; marriage with locals has proven effective in developing strong local ties. For example, Mokthar Belmokhtar, an Algerian AQIM leader, married a Tuareg woman, the daughter of one of the chiefs of the Arab Barabicha tribe in northern Mali.[127] AQIM has cast itself as an ally and protector of the local community. Regardless, the marriage of convenience or "joint offensive" that existed between AQIM and the MNLA in late 2011 and early 2012 seems to have soured in the aftermath of the coup. Each group had a starkly different—and incompatible—vision for northern Mali.

Salafi Islam was imposed by force, through AQIM and its allies, Ansar Dine and MUJAO, during the campaign for control over the northern cities. By June 2012, Islamist forces had seized control of the region's three major cities: Kidal, Gao, and Timbuktu. In Gao, for example, Ansar Dine imposed dress regulations on women, including female doctors in the hospital, part of their enforcement of a strict version of Islamic law.[128] There appeared to be very close ties between Ansar Dine and AQIM, the AQIM presence in areas controlled by Ansar Dine been described as an everyday reality, and senior AQIM leaders including Belmokhtar, Abou Zeid, and Nabil Abu Alqama were seen in Timbuktu shortly after the city fell to Ansar Dine.[129]

Ansar Dine, also known as "Defenders of the Faith," rose out of a splintering inside the Tuareg nationalist movement. The group was founded in November 2011 and led by the influential Tuareg nationalist leader, Iyad ag Ghali. Ag Ghali had become a follower of the fundamentalist Islamist group, Tabligh I Jumaat, and was subsequently sidelined by the broader nationalist movement.[130] Ag Ghali rejected the MNLA goal of independence, instead stating that the imposition of sharia, rather than independence should be the primary goal.[131]

Though Ansar Dine is estimated to have only 300 followers, its influence on life in areas under its control was great, with reports of:

> ordering women to wear veils and respect Islamic law. They have been going to hairdressers and ripping down photos of unveiled women, shutting down brothels and prohibiting the sale of alcoholic drinks.[132]

Despite their differences, Ansar Dine signed an agreement brokered by Algeria with the MNLA in late-May 2012 to cooperate and work together to create an independent Islamic state on the territory they occupy, stating both sides had made concessions.[133] Only a few days later, the merger was rejected by MNLA over the issue of Shari'a.[134] The MNLA ultimately dropped its demand for independence and entered into peace negotiations with the Malian government in December 2012. In January 2013, they welcomed the French military intervention in the north, offering support on the ground, declaring: "We can do the job on the ground. We've got men, arms and, above all, the desire to rid Azawad of terrorism."[135]

AQIM, itself, was not immune to splintering. In 2011, some younger members of AQIM broke off to form the MUJAO. There may also be an ethnic dimension to the split as MUJOA's leadership is made up of black Africans, leading to speculation they resented domination by AQIM's Arab leadership. Still others have suggested the split was a result of suspicions that AQIM had been infiltrated by Algerian security services. Sharing the same goals as AQIM, MUJAO has been very active in kidnapping for ransom.[136] In November 2012, MUJAO claimed to have ousted the MNLA rebels from Menaka.[137]

The speed at which Islamist forces were able to consolidate their hold over the cities in the north and begin to push into other areas factored into France's decision to take action rather than awaiting the arrival of regional force. In December 2012, the UN authorized deployment of an African-led security force to Mali, providing a legal international mandate for the use of force in Mali. The AFISMA was to be composed of forces, drawn primarily from ECOWAS countries, with a 1-year mandate.[138] However, creation of the force would take time and their level of capability was a concern. According to the French foreign minister, "France had little choice but to intervene urgently or Islamist forces might have made it to Bamako. . . ."[139]

On January 11, 2013, French air strikes on Mali launched Operation SERVAL. France deployed nearly 4,000 troops to Mali, including Special Forces. Working alongside Malian troops, they quickly forced the Islamists out of the region's major cities. Troops from neighboring Chad also deployed, taking heaving casualties in the fight for Kidal.[140] The cost of Operation SERVAL as of April 16, 2013, had reached €205 million. The total included €91 million for strategic transport, €55 million for personnel and €59 million in miscellaneous costs.[141] The United States provided logistical, technical, and intelligence support to Operation SERVAL, including air tankers to refuel French jets and transport planes.[142] Though the Barack Obama administration had initially declared they would not provide any ground troops in support of the French April 2013 operation, they confirmed they had deployed a small number of troops (approximately 22) in non-combat liaison roles to French and African troops.[143] In addition, the United States provided air tanker refuelers and transport planes.[144] Deciding intervention was in its national interests, Canada provided a C-17 aircraft, 25 percent of Operation SERVAL's strategic lift, to transport French armored vehicles, trucks, and troops.[145]

France began to withdraw its force in April 2013 and plans to have no more than 1,000 troops in the country by the end of 2013. Their duties are transitioning to the regional African force, AFISMA, which numbered approximately 6,300 in late April.[146] The size of the force, following the approval of a revised concept of operations by the African Union's (AU) Peace and Security Council, will be 9,620 personnel, including 171 civilians, 590 police officers, and 8,859 military personnel.[147] However, it will take some time for AFISMA to reach full deployment. Discussions over the size and status of the force are ongoing. Mali, with the support of ECOWAS and the African Union, requested the UN transition the force to a peacekeeping operation when possible. A subsequent report by the UN Secretary General ruled out this option, instead proposing either:

> . . . beefing-up the current multidimensional presence in Bamako and transforming it into an integrated political presence with a better resourced AFISMA. AFISMA would then have "an offensive combat and stabilisation mandate, focusing on extremist armed groups," together with bilateral military efforts. AFISMA would then transition to a UN stabilisation mission once certain critical benchmarks are met. The second option advocates for an integrated stabilisation mission with a military strength of 11,200 under Chapter VII alongside a parallel force to conduct counterterrorism operations beyond the scope of the UN's mandate.[148]

While much of the focus right now is on AFISMA and stabilization of the northern part of Mali, there is an urgent need to examine the overall regional security framework and the U.S. role in it. At the time of the March 2012 coup, the United States had spent nearly a decade developing a regional security framework. The coup, and the speed at with AQIM was able to capitalize on it, illustrate the fragility of this framework. Part III explores the weaknesses of the regional framework and identifies issues and challenges that will impact on creating a robust regional security framework.

PART III: THE SAHEL REGIONAL SECURITY FRAMEWORK

With the exception of Nigeria, a significant source of U.S. oil, the United States had little strategic interest in West Africa, and the Sahel in general, before September 11, 2001 (9/11). The U.S. regional security framework in the North African Sahel was born out of post-9/11 concerns that the region could be a possible haven for members of the transnational al-Qaeda network. Under the Global War on Terror paradigm, Africa, with its poor governance, ethnic conflict, extreme poverty, and the availability of ungoverned spaces could become "fertile breeding grounds for transnational Islamist terror."[149]

In 2002, the U.S. State Department launched the Pan Sahel Initiative (PSI), which later evolved into the Trans Sahara Counter Terrorism Partnership (TSCTP) program. In its first year, the Pan Sahel Initiative spent $6.25 million to conduct training and capacity building in Niger, Mali, Chad, and Mauritania. These partner military forces received training from the U.S. Marines and Army Special Forces and were provided tactical equipment such as night vision goggles.[150]

A defining moment that reinforced the need for a well-planned and coordinated regional effort against counterterrorism in the Sahel was the response to the 2003 kidnapping of 32 European hostages by AQIM's predecessor, the GSPC. The ensuing transnational gun battle went from Mali to Niger to Chad. The hunt for the GSPC leader, the Algerian paratrooper Amari Saifi known as "El Para," involved troops from Mali, Niger, Algeria, and Chad, with support from the United States European Command (EUCOM).[151]

The creation of the TSCTP in 2005 further expanded the extent of the regional security framework, while increasing focus on the underlying socioeconomic and political issues that drive violence and instability. A collaboration between the U.S. State Department and U.S. Department of Defense (DoD), the TSCTP:

> supports African states' efforts to improve border security and counterterrorism capacity while also facilitating regional cooperation, promoting democratic governance, and improving relations with the US.[152]

The regional framework was expanded to include Algeria, Nigeria, Morocco, Tunisia, and Senegal. With an anticipated budget of $100 million for 2007-13, the TSCTP is more heavily funded than the PSI, though the resources pale in comparison with the vastness of the continent. The TSCTP also reflects a shift, at least rhetorically, to a more comprehensive or whole-of-government approach toward terrorism that includes development initiatives. While military operations were still to be a major focus, emphasis was placed on increasing collaboration above the tactical level. Other government agencies, such as the U.S. Agency for International Development (USAID) and the Department of Treasury were to address underlying issues ranging from educational opportunities to money-handling controls, caused the program to be renamed the Trans Saharan Counter Terrorism Initiative.[153]

The military training exercise Flintlock launched the TSCTP in 2005. Flintlock is directed by the Chairman of the Joint Chiefs of Staff, sponsored by AFRICOM and the Joint Special Operations Task Force, and conducted by the TSCTP and Special Operations Forces. This multinational exercise regularly draws participants from 16 countries, including those from the Sahel region as well as Canada and European states. Flintlock 2012, scheduled for February 27-March 18 in Mali, was to emphasize military support to humanitarian assistance operation. It was cancelled February 10 due to ongoing clashes between government forces and rebel in the country's north.[154] The smaller annual exercise, Atlas Accord, took place in Mopti, Mali, from February 7-15, 2012. The exercise focused on enhancing air drop capabilities and drew more than 300 participants from seven countries.[155]

Organizationally, TSCTP was part of the EUCOM's Operation ENDURING FREEDOM, Trans Sahel (OEF-TS). In 2008, the TSCTP was transferred to the newly established AFRICOM. The creation of AFRICOM in 2007 reflects the U.S. Government's militarization of its relationship with African governments in the last decade. At its establishment, AFRICOM was touted for its potential capacity building and humanitarian role in Africa, the White House emphasized its ability to keep the peace through security cooperation:

> Africa Command will enhance our efforts to bring peace and security to the people of Africa and promote our common goals of development, health, education, democracy, and economic growth in Africa.[156]

Despite such statements, which intended to quell African concern over the growing U.S. military presence on the continent, AFRICOM's focus has been overwhelmingly on tactical level counterterrorism activities:

> . . . the Department of Defense's (DoD) most significant endeavors in Africa have been undertaken in pursuit of narrowly conceived goals related to the Global

War on Terrorism (GWOT). Operations in North and East Africa, though couched in a larger framework of development, long-term counterinsurgency, and a campaign to win "hearts and minds," have nonetheless relied on offensive military operations focused on short-term objectives.[157]

In short, the U.S. regional security framework for the Sahel has focused heavily on increasing local militaries capabilities to conduct direct action, not building long-term community and national level institutional capacity and resiliency to combat violent extremism or the development of strong national governance. Debate continues over the appropriateness of a rather broad and ambiguous peace and security role for AFRICOM and the portrayal of it mission as "preventative." Critics note that it is "highly plausible" that AFRICOM will use it full combatant command functions to respond to threats or crises on the continent, selling it as a preventative force creates the potential for backlash should that occur.[158]

Beyond failing to systematically address the drivers of conflict and extremism, some critics argue that increasing the ability of African partner governments to suppress terrorism within their own borders may have had the unintended consequence of increasing U.S. enemies. Such new counterterrorism capabilities have been used to repress local Muslim social and political organizations that have no link to al-Qaeda in an effort to reduce political challenges.[159] Counterterrorism capabilities and participation in the U.S.-led GWOT can be used by those in power to settle long-standing scores against groups or individuals, a potential factor in the recent Mali crisis.

In his testimony before the Senate Committee on Foreign Relations, David Gutelius, a consulting senior fellow at Johns Hopkins University, described the situation in Mali:

> From the beginning in 2003, key Tamashek and Arab populations were largely left out of PSI-sponsored activities, exacerbating the long-standing ill-will between these groups and the national governments of Niger and Mali. This fact, combined with the rhetoric U.S. officials and their local allies used at the time very quickly brought out older tensions and suspicions, and linked them to the U.S. military.[160]

Indeed, the U.S. focus on capacity building to meet the transnational threat emanating from Mali may have worsened an internal political situation that ultimately contributed to the overthrow of the civilian government. A more multifaceted concept of security threats, to include the role of effective and legitimate national governance on internal stability, should be the basis for the future, multidimensional, regional security framework. Such a framework, however, will face numerous challenges, many of which cannot be addressed through the use of military means alone.

Challenges of The Regional Security Framework in the Sahel.

Differing Priorities among Framework Members.

Differing priorities, and the lack of a common view of the threat, will continue to challenge the creation of a robust security framework in the Sahel region and the partnerships that will sustain it. The United States has held a far too narrow definition of African security interests; one that often conflicts directly with the security priorities held by most African states. While the threat of transnational violent extremism first drew the interest of the United States and remains its absolute priority, it is typically not the national priority of their partner countries. In these countries, the threats posed by corruption, poor growth, and internal instability, in addition to threats from armed groups, are, by pragmatism and necessity, often of far greater concern. In 2002, the AU established the New Partnership for African Development (NEPAD), which established a vision and strategic framework for Africa's future. Its action plan established four broad priorities for Africa:

> peace and security, democracy and governance, regional co-operation and integration, and capacity building. In addition, the framework highlights eight sectoral priorities, including: agriculture, human development, infrastructure, intra-African trade market access and the environment.[161]

This is not to say that the regional framework did not ever address U.S. priorities, however, the cooperation has been described as ad hoc and inhibited by a range of regional tensions. For example, in 2010, Algeria, Mauritania, Mali, and Niger created the Joint Military Command in Tamanrasset, Algeria, to operationalize counterterrorism cooperation. Algeria and Mauritania conducted operations in Mali and Algeria and even provided Mali with training and equipment to fight AQIM. However, by January 2012, Algeria had withdrawn its cooperation in an effort to get Mali to address the Tuareg issue.[162]

With the current deployment of AFISMA and ECOWAS troops into Mali, the regional security framework has undergone a de facto expansion — and now includes a far broader range of countries. While this expanded framework brings benefits, not least of which is an African solution to the Mali crisis, it will increase the challenge of coordination and consensus building. These countries, too, are constrained by their national priorities. The Ivory Coast (Côte d'Ivoire) is struggling to recover from a decade-long civil war, while Guinea's politics are marked by coups and cancelled elections. Nigeria, which at 1,200 troops is making one of the largest contributions to AFISMA, faces a growing conflict between the government and the Islamic militant group, Boko Haram, that will dominate its security concerns.

Two thousand Chadian troops played a significant role in Operation SERVAL. Long an ally of France, Chad, at 1,800 troops, is also a major contributor to AFISMA and will likely expand its role in the region's security framework. But Chad faces its own internal challenges. In May 2013, two senior generals, among others, were arrested for plotting a coup; though critics contend the government's actions were to suppress opponents of President Idriss Deby.[163]

When the crisis broke, Mauritania reinforced its border with Mali, helping to contain the situation. But Mauritania also faces increasing protests by the Democratic Opposition Coordinating Body, which is calling for President Mohamed Ould Abdel Aziz and his government to step down.[164]

While not an exhaustive list, these are representative of the issues that will compete with the priorities of a regional security framework.

Lack of Long Term Partnerships.

The lack of long-term alliances with many of the countries in the region hampered a rapid and robust U.S. response to regional threats emanating from there. Today, it is well understood within the DoD that "You can't surge trust. You must build it slowly and deliberately before a crisis occurs."[165] Any regional framework must rest on the creation of long-term partnerships, however, both budgetary constraints and higher priority security issues in other regions will undermine sustained focus on the Sahel.

Prior to 9/11, U.S. bilateral relations in North Africa focused primarily on Egypt, not the Maghreb, with a notable exception of Morocco. Much of North Africa and the Sahel has long been part of a French sphere of influence on the continent, and the United States has few deep commercial or economic ties. Similarly, in West Africa, U.S. relations have focused primarily on Nigeria, a major source of U.S. oil supplies and Senegal, which participated in Operation DESERT STORM. When the need arose to address the AQIM threat, the United States did not have a network of deep partnerships, especially at the military-to-military level, to draw on in the region; the gaps and seams in this network undermined the overall efficacy of the security framework.

While the United States has had a long-standing diplomatic relationship with many countries in the Sahel zone, the focus was typically on humanitarian and development aid, not military cooperation. With the notable exception of Morocco, deep bilateral military-to-military relationships in North Africa and the Sahel, especially with French speaking countries are also a post-9/11 phenomenon. The United States and Algeria, for example, conducted their first formal joint military dialogue in Washington, DC, in May 2005.

Following 9/11, the George Bush administration launched a major policy aimed at creating a deeper network of relations in the region in order to address global terrorism. The Middle East Partnership Initiative (MEPI) focused on democratization, in addition to economic growth, education, and women's development. The political overtones of this initiative complicated efforts to build these relationships as regional governments were resistant to externally imposed political reform. It did not help that the MEPI program was launched at the same time that the United States invaded Iraq, an event that was to unleash a "democratic tsunami" in the region. The timing sent a message to the region's leaders that they could face the same outcome and increased resistance to externally imposed political reform.[166] Though MEPI's budget has increased over time, it was initially poorly resourced, signifying that, despite rhetoric, the region and its role in GWOT were not a priority. The extent of the disparity between funds to fight war and money to prevent potential conflict was noted in a congressional hearing on MEPI by Representative (New York) Eliot Engel:

> I find it ironic, almost surreal, that we are here discussing a program designed to help foster democratization in the Middle East through an incrementalist program just as our troops are poised to invade Iraq and bring democracy there forcefully. We look at the budget. We have $145 million for the Middle East Peace Initiative, and we have $145 billion for war and rebuilding in Iraq.[167]

Indeed, more pressing issues in Iraq and Afghanistan, and later the Horn of Africa, continued to draw increasingly scarce U.S. financial and diplomatic resources away from potential initiatives in the Sahel.

The long adversarial relationship with Libyan ruler Muammar Gaddafi excluded it from the U.S.-led regional security framework. The antagonism extended for decades, fueled by Gaddafi's nationalization of oil companies in 1972, the Gulf of Sidra incident and Libya's role in the downing of the airliner PAN AM 103 over Lockerbie, Scotland. Though the United States and Libya began a normalization process prior to the Libyan revolution in 2011, it was not involved in formal mechanisms of the U.S. regional security framework. As a result, the framework had a crucial and critical gap. Sharing a long border with Algeria, perhaps the closest U.S. partner in the region today, and having a long-term relationship with the Tuaregs, Libya was a major player in the regional security framework, even if the United States did not wish to acknowledge it. In addition to his support for the Tuareg and their integration into his military, Gaddafi also used his oil wealth to pay for essential services in neighboring countries, giving him considerable influence and reach. Burkina Faso, for example, offered him exile at the time of the Libyan revolution.

The demise of Gaddafi's regime, hastened by the NATO-led Operation UNIFIED PROTECTOR, was a catalyst that drove the events leading to the crisis in northern Mali. While the Libyan revolution may eventually lead to the development of a stable government with civil society participation, its current instability in the short term, and the potential for Libya itself to develop into a safe haven will dramatically impact the region's future security framework.

Competing Interests and Capabilities Among Regional Partners.

Within the TSCTP regional framework, the differing interests, priorities, and capabilities of the member states can undermine the effectiveness of the overall framework. In light of AQIM's Algerian roots, Mali views them as an Algerian problem, and has doubts about Algeria's level of cooperation. Conversely, Algeria sees Mali as the weak link in the chain, not committed to dealing with AQIM.[168] Indeed, the state of relations between Algeria and Mali has been described as a "rupture of the strategic alliance" during President Touré's term. This situation undermined security cooperation to the advantage of both AQIM and Ansar Dine. To avoid getting drawn into an internal conflict between the Tuareg and the government, Algeria did not intervene when the rebels took the strategic border town of Tessalit and did not help Malian forces hold Kidal, despite the General Staff Joint Operations Committee (CEMOC) of the region's countries (Mali, Mauritania, Niger, and Algeria) being based in Tamanrasset, southern Algeria.[169]

At the same time, Algeria has long played a role in mediating between Mali and the Tuareg, promoting a political solution. In 2008, they negotiated a short-lived peace deal. Algeria has also played a key role in the development of regional counterterrorism capability, providing military support to Mali, including logistics, training, and equipment, especially along their shared border. Algeria has given Malian soldiers, both officers and noncommissioned officers, access to Algerian military schools. In January 2012, Algeria temporarily froze military support to Mali after Mali suspended counterterror operations in Gao, Kidal, and Timbuktu to focus on addressing the Tuareg rebellion. At the same time, Algeria launched a diplomatic effort to mediate between the MNLA and the Malian government.[170] Algerian diplomats reportedly tried to pressure the Tuareg into talks. Algeria refused to treat wounded MNLA fighters, instead insisting on maintaining its neutral stance in the conflict.[171]

Distrust, especially over the disputed Western Sahel territory, has long characterized the Algerian-Moroccan relationship. Algeria has accused Morocco of hosting and supporting the Armed Islamic Group of Algeria, an accusation Morocco denies.[172] Conversely, some Moroccan officials have accused Algeria of involvement in the 1994 Marrakesh bombing. These tensions led to the closing of their shared border in 1994; it remains closed.

While Algeria is often concerned that the actions of its neighbors are counter to Algerian interests and keeps a wary eye on partnerships such as French-Niger cooperation, it also does not want to be excluded from regional alliances. Algeria is not part of ECOWAS and is not a participant in AFISMA. However, Algerian permission to overfly its territory was crucial to the success of Operation SERVAL.[173]

Memories of the Algerian War of Independence always overshadow the Algerian-French relationship. The war, much of which took the form of an urban guerilla campaign, lasted from 1954 until Algeria's independence in 1962. Estimates of Algerian casualties range from 1 to 1.5 million; the French lost over 25,000, with another 65,000 wounded. There is enormous sensitivity inside Algeria to the idea of French military deployment on their border. In the run up to Operation SERVAL, Algeria pushed for a political, not military, solution to the problem of northern Mali.

Differing Levels of Military Capability among the Partners.

Among the countries in the regional framework, Algeria's military, with a force of 147,000 (127,000 active duty) and a budget exceeding $5 billion a year, is by far the largest, and likely the most well-trained.[174] As Warner notes:

> Having fought insurgency and terrorism since the early 1990s, Algeria's military was also one of the strongest, most capable and most battle-hardened in the region.[175]

Other regional forces are much smaller in comparison. Even Chad, which actively participated in Operation SERVAL and has had a number of notable counter-terrorism successes, has a force of only 23,350 and a budget of $436 million. With a strength of 7,750 troops (before the coup) and a budget of $174 million, Mali and Niger (5,300 troops, $53.1 million budget) have few resources to control their vast territories.[176]

In a very real sense, Mali's current crisis is — at least in part — a result of Algeria's counterterrorism success, especially its activities in remote Kabylie Mountains. There, in the fall of 2012, the local Berbers population began to turn against AQIM. Frustrated by the impact of kidnappings on their essential tourist economy, they began to assist security forces and provide them with information leading to the capture or killing of militants. The most significant event was the October 14 killing of Bekkai Boualem, also known as Khaled El Mig, the head of external relations for AQIM, by security forces.[177] Their success pushed AQIM further south, into northern Mali.

Such a "whack-a-mole" approach is also reflected in the level and type of training provided by the United States to its regional partners, which focused overwhelmingly on tactical level capabilities. There seems to have been little attention to strategic level considerations and the linkages between the three levels of war. Operational considerations, such as how residents of northern Mali, including the Tuareg, would perceive the U.S. and Malian government counterterrorism cooperation, seem to have been overlooked or ignored.

Though a key element of the military-to-military engagement was to promote professionalism and deference to civilian authority, the coup in Mali was led by a U.S. trained officer, Captain Sandogo. This fact, and the human rights violations by Malian forces, suggests that more training is needed in this area. According to General Carter F. Ham, former commander of AFRICOM:

> From a purely military standpoint, U.S. forces focused Malian training almost exclusively on tactical and technical matters such as operating equipment, improving tactical effectiveness and aerial re-supply to remote bases. All of which is very, very good, we didn't spend, probably, the requisite time focusing on values, ethics and military ethos.[178]

In the future, development of the regional security framework should broaden to include a focus on security sector reform, including strengthening the civilian institutions that uphold the rule of law, not just security force assistance and tactical level capabilities. Here, African institutions such as the AU and ECOWAS may be able to take the lead or provide a substantial supporting role. The AU developed a common Security Sector Reform framework, and ECOWAS adopted the *Code of Conduct for the Armed Forces and Security*

Services in West Africa. Again, increasing security force capability without institutional development reform could worsen the situation in Mali.[179]

However, ECOWAS' mandate in Mali, and its troops' capabilities, is limited. AFISMA is initially authorized to operate only for 1 year, until December 2013. Much of that time will be spent organizing and deploying the troops. Critics in the UN and Europe describe ECOWAS' initial plan for deployment as confused and inadequate, a factor that led to France's action.

The internal chaos in Mali further complicates the deployment of AFISMA troops. Following the coup, the Malian military broke up into various factions, leaving ECOWAS with no single representative to coordinate and define the military mission. The armies of ECOWAS also have primary expertise in forested terrain, not the arid terrain of the Sahel.

The Sahel's Increasing Vulnerability to Humanitarian Crisis.

During the crisis in northern Mali, Mali and the surrounding countries faced a severe humanitarian crisis that was rooted in long-term food insecurity issues and worsened by increasing flows of refugees fleeing conflict areas. In April 2012, the Food and Agriculture Organization estimated that:

> more than 16 million people were facing food security issues including more than 1 million children under the age of five who are at risk of severe acute malnutrition, putting them at risk of death from starvation or disease in the Sahel Region of Western Africa.[180]

In Mali, 178,000 children were at risk, 330,000 in Niger, 127,000 in Chad, and 208,000 in Northern Nigeria.[181]

After the coup and increase in fighting in the north, few humanitarian organizations were able to remain in the area and provide services. The United Nations had no presence during the conflict. The FAO issued a warning for Mali:

> The humanitarian situation, particularly for pastoralists, **is a matter of very deep concern as insecurity worsens in Mali and the food supply is disrupted. Extreme food insecurity or localized famine situations cannot be excluded if this situation lasts two or three additional months.** (Emphasis in original.) [182]

Historically, food insecurity and famine among the Tuareg is linked to periods of mobilization among the population for anti-government action. A hunger crisis and the government's inability to address it adequately could lead to additional support for the Tuareg rebels and increased calls for independence.[183]

Fighting in the north also created a refugee crisis. As of February 2013, there were 260,665 estimated internal displaced persons in Mali. Of these, 76,500 were located in the north (Timbuktu, Gao, and Kidal), as many others fled south during the conflict.[184] Malians, including large numbers of Tuaregs, also fled to neighboring countries. In June 2013, there were an estimated 170,000 refugees in Burkina Faso (49,975), Mauritania (74,108), and Niger (50,000).[185] Issues such as these are, according to General Ham, "patently the most difficult to address."

In the aftermath of Operation SERVAL, some refugees and internally displaced persons have begun to return to their homes, and nongovernmental organizations now have access. However, the impact of the conflict will linger, and as of June 2013, northern Mali remained classified as a food crisis area. It will take time for trade and market activity to recover. As many of the most well-off families, who had provided jobs for other members of society, fled, economic opportunities became scarce.[186] Even beyond the current crisis, Mali faces long-term food security issues that can create dissatisfaction among the population. If the state cannot meet their needs, others will exploit this gap.

Over the longer term, Mali must also deal with the effects of climate change.[187] The rise of water temperatures in Gulf of Guinea has shifted flow of rain clouds southwards, causing even greater dryness in the Sahel. Drought has severely impacted cereal production across the region. In Niger, the cereal harvest was more than 25 percent smaller in 2011 than in previous years. Niger faces a shortfall of 500,000 tons of grain, a situation worse than the previous crises in 2005 and 2010.[188] In Mali, grain production has fallen by 41 percent compared to 2011.[189] Indeed, the northern Sahel region has faced three droughts in the last 10 years.

Mali's average annual rainfall has decreased 30 percent since 1998; droughts are longer and more common. Desertification, where land is becoming increasingly arid, is also a problem in Mali where the Sahara is moving southward at a rate of 48-km (30 miles) a year.[190] As a result of the Sahara's southern movement, Mali is experiencing climate zone shift. This shift will bring additional negative consequences to Mali. According to 22 global climate models that forecast to 2030, the most negative scenario could mean a decrease in rainfall by 10 percent and an increase in average temperatures by 1.8 degrees Fahrenheit. This scenario would result in a $300 million agricultural loss for Mali; even under the most optimistic climate models, annuals losses of $120 million are forecast.[191] This anticipated climate change will put even greater strains on the population and society in northern Mali, and increase the potential for instability that can be exploited by criminals and militants.

Internal Stability in Mali.

Finally, Mali's own internal political and security issues prevented it from becoming a reliable partner in any regional security framework, at least until the current interim government was replaced with a permanent one. Any new government in Mali may face a potential protracted conflict with AQIM and associated groups. Though French and African forces were able to quickly clear the cities, many of the militants melted away in to the desert and highlands, and likely across borders, where they may regroup and plan new attacks.

In a foreboding sign that liberated Mali might descend into insurgency, in February 2013, MUJAO militants used canoes to cross the Niger river and infiltrate Gao, launching three separate attacks on Malian and French troops. Two of the attacks were suicide bombings. No French or Malian soldiers were killed, though one Malian soldier was wounded.[192] A few months later in May 2013, two Malian soldiers were killed by a suicide bomber in Gao.[193]

Also recovered in northern Mali was a copy of an AQAP-authored document containing 22 ways to avoid drone detection/attacks. Options range from the low tech, such as the use of reflective pieces of glass on roof of car or building or hiding under trees trees, to high tech, including the use of Russian-made sky grabber device to infiltrate the drone's waves and the frequencies. The device is available in the market for $2,595.[194] Though it is unclear how successful such tactics are against drones' electronic countermeasures, the document illustrates information sharing across the al-Qaeda network and the potential for low technology approaches to facilitate sustainment of long-term conflict in the region. To build security in the north long-term security sector reform and political legitimacy are essential.

The institution of a new government recognized as legitimate by the country as a whole is an absolute requirement for Mali to be able to address the security situation in the north. It is not clear if that will happen. In December 2012, prime minister Cheick Modibo Derra and his cabinet resigned abruptly, following his arrest by a soldier. The country's military leadership accused him of playing a personal agenda.[195]

Presidential elections, originally scheduled for April 2013, took place in July and August 2013. Despite the challenges posed by geography, severe weather, and security issues, the electoral process was largely considered to be credible. Ibrahim Boubacar Keita, often referred to as IBK, won the presidency in a second round of voting. He and his opponent, Soumaila Cissé, received the most votes of the 27 candidates that stood in the first round of voting. Keita served as Mali's prime minister from 1994 to 2000. The successful election will allow Mali to access $4 billion in aid from international donors that was suspended following the coup.[196]

A new government will have to be constructed against a backdrop of growing ethnic tensions unleashed during the conflict in the north. During the conflict, Malians of Arab or Tuareg descent were looted or harassed, targeted on the basis of their physical appearance. Malian soldiers have been accused of such targeting and committing atrocities against those from the north. According to one report, "People with fair skin (notably Tuaregs and Arabs) no longer use buses to travel between the north and the south."[197] Long simmering tensions have now erupted and will need to be addressed if there is to be stability in the long term.

President Keita has stated that a lasting peace deal — a real peace with the Tuareg — is his first priority. According to a ceasefire that allowed voting to take place in northern Mali, Keita's government must open talks with the Tuaregs within 60 days. Any chance for long-term stability of Mali rests on the successful conclusion of an agreement and its implementation.[198]

CONCLUSION

While there is no doubt that the presence of AQIM in northern Mali is a counterterrorism problem for the United States, the solutions to the crisis in Mali are as much political and economic, if not more so, than military. Long-term stability and resiliency against militant Islamic extremism depends on an approach in which the indirect lines of operation, such as economic development, strengthening of political institutions, and the amelioration of the effects of climate change, work alongside the careful application of direct action against the threat of violent extremism.

This will be impossible to achieve without the full support of the new Malian government. The position the government adopts toward the Tuareg movements, both nationalist and religious, will determine the likelihood of bringing long-term stability to Mali. Should the government decide that it will not negotiate with Ansar Dine, this will severely complicate efforts to normalize the north and will allow for the continuation of grievances than can again be exploited by AQIM. Similarly, in their joint support for Operation SERVAL, the secular, nationalist Tuaregs and the Malian government found themselves on the same side of an issue. Though unplanned, this alignment offers the opportunity for renewed negotiation on the status of the Tuareg and the conditions in the north of the country.

U.S. policymakers should adopt a more multidimensional view of security in Mali, and indeed, Africa overall. While countering violent extremists must remain a priority, increased emphasis should be focused on the issues that create the safe havens in which they hide. Physical security, often secured through military and law enforcement efforts, is a prerequisite for the development of institutions of good governance. Without such institutions physical security is fleeting and needs constant intervention when a crisis erupts.

Building stability in Mali will require a long-term, focused commitment of money and diplomatic effort. Such costs are difficult to justify, especially at a time when the United States and its European allies face enormous economic challenges. However, the investment in social, political, and economic development to address the underlying or "upstream" factors that lead to instability may be a far less expensive option than paying for military intervention when a crisis erupts. In the 5 years before the coup, the United States provided about $400 million in civilian assistance programs to Mali. The first 6 months of Operation UNIFIED PROTECTOR in Libya, however, cost the United States $1 billion.[199] While military assistance was not responsible for the crisis in Mali, the balance between military and civilian forms of assistance in creating overall security should be given serious consideration. Long-term persistent partnerships with key partner nations must integrate any counterterrorism campaign into a multidimensional approach to security that seeks to address diverse types of threats and potential threats.

ENDNOTES

1. Office of the Press Secretary, Statement by the Press Secretary on Mali, Washington, DC, The White House, March 22, 2012, available from *www.whitehouse.gov/the-press-office/2012/03/22/statement-press-secretary-mali*.

2. Lyrics from the group, Tinariwen, available from *www.tinariwen.com/tassili-lyrics/*.

3. In 2009, the Obama administration requested the term "Global War on Terror" be replaced with the "long war" or, more commonly, "overseas contingency operation." See Scott Wilson and Al Kamen, "'Global War on Terror' is Given a New Name," *The Washington Post*, March 25, 2009, available from *articles.washingtonpost.com/2009-03-25/politics/36918330_1_congressional-testimony-obama-administration-memo*.

4. Atlas Accord, available from *www.africom.mil/what-we-do/exercises/atlas-accord*.

5. United Nations Security Council Resolution (UNSCR) 2085, passed in December 2012, authorized deployment of an African-led International Support Mission to Mali. Earlier resolutions, UNSC 2056 called for the restoration of constitutional order. UNSCR 2071 authorized the African Union (AU) and the Economic Community of West African States (ECOWAS) to plan for military intervention in Mali. UNSCR 2085 available from *www.un.org/News/Press/docs/2012/sc10870.doc.htm*.

6. David Lewis, "Analysis: Mali Coup Shakes Cocktail of Instability in Sahel," *Reuters*, March 24, 2012.

7. Anne Gearan and Craig Whitlock, "Panetta 'Confident' that U.S. Will Clear Legal Hurdles to Helping France in Mali," *The Washington Post*, January 16, 2013.

8. "US Military Sending Air Tankers to Refuel French Jets Over Mali," *The Guardian* (UK), January 27, 2013, available from *www.guardian.co.uk/world/2013/jan/27/us-military-tankers-french-mali*.

9. Adam Entous and Siobhan Gorman, "US to Expand Role in Africa," *The Wall Street Journal*, January 28, 2013, available from *online.wsj.com/article/SB1000142412788732364490457827037413070 8196.html*.

10. In April 2012, the United States suspended $13 million of its $140 million dollar aid program for Mali. Programs cut included health services, school construction, and agricultural development, see "US Suspends $13 Million in Aid to Mali," *Reuters*, April 4, 2012, available from *www.reuters.com/article/2012/04/05/us-mali-usa-idUSBRE83402P20120405*. Section 7008 of the Fiscal Year (FY)2012 Consolidated Appropriations Act, P.L. 112-74, bars State Department and USAID-administered aid to the government of any country in which a military coup or decree has overthrown a democratically elected government. For additional information on cuts to the U.S. security assistance program for Mali, see Alexis Arieff, "Crisis in Mali," *CRS Report for Congress*, January 14, 2013, available from *www.fas.org/sgp/crs/row/R42664.pdf*.

11. "Mali Facts," *National Geographic*, available from *travel.nationalgeographic.com/travel/countries/mali-facts/#*.

12. Mali data (2011) retrieved from the World Bank, *"World Development Indicators,"* available from *available from data.worldbank.org/country/mali*.

13. *Central Intelligence Agency (CIA) World Factbook*, "Mali."

14. *Ibid.*

15. For a detailed analysis of Tuareg pastoral systems and the various Tuareg confederations, see Edmond Bernus, "Dates Dromedaries and Drought: Diversification in Tuareg Pastoralist

Systems," in John. G. Galaty and Douglas L. Johnson, eds. *The World of Pastoralism Herding Systems in Comparative Perspective*, New York: Guilford, 1990, pp. 149-176, available from *horizon. documentation.ird.fr/exl-doc/pleins_textes/pleins_textes_6/b_fdi_33-34/38699.pdf*.

16. Antonio Guterres, "Why Mali Matters," *The New York Times* (Opinion), September 4, 2012, available from *www.nytimes. com/2012/09/05/opinion/why-mali-matters.html?_r=0*.

17. Angelia Sanders and Samuel Lau, *Al Qaeda and the African Arc of Instability*, Norfolk VA: Allied Command Operation (ACO) Civil Military Fusion Center, 2012, available from *www.cimicweb. org/cmo/medbasin/Holder/Documents/r025%20CFC%20Monthly%20 Thematic%20Report%20(03-JAN-13).pdf*.

18. "Revealed Al-Qaeda's 22 Tips for Dodging Drones," *The Telegraph* (United Kingdom), February 21, 2013, available from *www.telegraph.co.uk/news/worldnews/al-qaeda/9886637/Revealed-al-Qaedas-22-tips-for-dodging-drones.html*.

19. "The Al-Qaida Papers—Drones," *The Associated Press*, no date, available from *hosted.ap.org/specials/interactives/_international/_pdfs/al-qaida-papers-drones.pdf*.

20. "Africa's arc of instability has myriad causes," *The Guardian* (United Kingdom) Opinion, January 19, 2013, available from *www.guardian.co.uk/commentisfree/2013/jan/20/observer-editorial-mali-algeria-western-response*.

21. Tyrone C. Marshall, "Africom Commander Addresses Concerns, Potential Solutions in Mali," *Armed Forces Press Service*, January 24, 2013, available from *www.defense.gov/news/newsarticle. aspx?id=119103*.

22. The Malian empire is also sometimes referred to as the Manden Kurufaba.

23. For more information on Sijilmassa and the Saharan trade route network, see Dale R. Lightfoot and James Miller, "'Sijilmas-sa': The Rise and Fall of a Walled Oasis in Medieval Morocco," *Annals of the Association of American Geographers*, Vol. 86, No. 1, March 1996, pp. 78-101.

24. For more on Ibn Battuta's travels, see Ross E. Dunn, *The Adventures of Ibn Battuta: A Muslim Traveler of the 14th Century*, Berkeley, CA: University of California Press, 2004.

25. Ibn Khaldun wrote that the Malian Empire experienced dynastic cycles in where a strong ruler would be followed by a good ruler but the quality of leadership would deteriorate by the third successor, causing a period of ineffective rule that would lead to the rise of a new strong ruler, and the dynastic cycle would start again. For details of Ibn Khaldun's theory, see Ralph A. Austen and Jan Jansen, "History, Oral Transmission and Structure in Ibn Khaldun's Chronology of Mali Rulers," *History in Africa*, Vol. 23, 1996, pp. 17-28, available from *https://openaccess.leidenuniv.nl/ bitstream/handle/1887/2778/1241586_032.pdf;jsessionid=060C3125B0 F319109C1572C1FFDF0A36?sequence=1.*

26. Thomas A. Hale, *Griots and Griottes: Masters of Words and Music*. Bloomington, IN: Indiana University Press, 1998.

27. "Mansa" is a term meaning emperor or ruler.

28. A. J. H. Goodwin, "The Medieval Empire of Ghana," *South African Archaeological Bulletin*, Vol. 12, 1957, pp. 108–112.

29. United Nations Educational Scientific and Cultural Organization (UNESCO), "Timbuktu," available from *whc.unesco.org/ en/list/119.*

30. See also Lydia Polgreen, "As Extremists Invaded, Timbuktu Hid Artifacts of a Golden Age," *The New York Times*, February 3, 2013, available from *www.nytimes.com/2013/02/04/world/ africa/saving-timbuktus-priceless-artifacts-from-militants-clutches. html?pagewanted=2&_r=0&pagewanted=print.*

31. Ishaan Tharour, "Mali's Crisis: Terror Stalks the History Treasures of Timbuktu," *Time*, April 5, 2012, available from *world.time.com/2012/04/05/malis-crisis-terror-stalks-the-historic- treasures-of-timbuktu/#ixzz2JrsZXbYO.*

32. Graziano Krätli, "The Book and the Sand: Restoring and Preserving the Ancient Desert Libraries of Mauritania—Part I," *World Libraries*, Vol. 14, No. 1, 2004.

33. "Timbuktu Mausoleums Destroyed," *British Broadcasting Corporation* (BBC), December 23, 2012, available from *www.bbc. co.uk/news/world-africa-20833010*.

34. Sufism is a moderate, spiritual, and mystical form of Islam that focuses on an individual's achievement of total commitment to God. Salafists such as Ansar Dine consider Sufism to be "unIslamic." "Mali fighters destroy more Timbuktu tombs," *Al Jazeera,* December 23, 2012, available from *www.aljazeera.com/ news/africa/2012/12/2012122317115353560.html*.

35. Luke Harding, "Timbuktu Mayor: Mali Rebels Torched Library of Historic Manuscripts," *The Guardian* (UK), January, 28, 2013, available from *www.guardian.co.uk/world/2013/jan/28/mali-timbuktu-library-ancient-manuscripts*.

36. Polgreen, "As Extremists Invaded."

37. Tristan McConnell, "How Timbuktu Saved its Books," *Harper's Magazine*, February 4, 2013, available from *harpers.org/ blog/2013/02/how-timbuktu-saved-its-book/*.

38. "Director-General visits Mali with French President Hollande," UNESCO, February 3, 2013, available from *www.unesco. org/new/en/unesco/resources/director-general-visits-mali-with-french-president-francois-hollande/*.

39. For more on the impact of the development of the compass, see Amir Aczel, *The Riddle of the Compass: The Invention that Changed the World*, New York: Harcourt Books, 2001.

40. By far the best description of the world system prior to the Age of Discovery is Janet Abu Lughod, *Before European Hegemony: The World System AD 1250-1350*, Oxford, UK: Oxford University Press, 1989. See, in particular, the final chapter on the restructuring of the 13th century world system.

41. The full title of the work is *Description de l'Égypte, ou Recueil des observations et des recherches qui ont été faites en Égypte pendant l'expédition de l'armée française* (*Description of Egypt, or the Collection of Observations and Research which Were Made in Egypt during the Expedition of the French Army*). The World Digital Library has

scanned digital copies of much of this work, available from *www. wdl.org/en/item/80/.*

42. Many of Burton's writings are in the public domain and available free in digital form. This includes his two-volume account of *West Africa: To the Gold Coast for Gold. A Personal Narrative* (1883).

43. Martin Dugard, "Stanley Meets Livingston," *The Smithsonian,* October 2003, available from *www.smithsonianmag.com/history-archaeology/livingstone.html.*

44. For an excellent, detailed account of European imperial expansion into Africa, see Thomas Pakenham, *The Scramble for Africa: White Man's Conquest of the Dark Continent from 1876-1912,* New York: Avon Books, 1991.

45. This area was originally called Upper Senegal in 1880 and renamed French Sudan in 1890. The territorial components of the French Sudan changed numerous times; at one time French Sudan split into Upper Senegal and Niger. By 1920, it was again called the French Sudan, and this name remained in use until Mali's independence in 1960.

46. Norman Dwight Harris: "French Colonial Expansion in West Africa, the Sudan and the Sahara," *The American Political Science Review,* Vol. 5, No. 3, 1911, pp 353-373.

47. The African Franc (CFA) replaced it in 1945 and is still used in Benin, Burkina Faso, Côte d'Ivoire, Guinuea-Bissau, Mali, Niger, Senegal, and Togo.

48. An English translation of Rene Caillie's book, *Travels Through Central Africa to Timbuctoo: and Across the Great Desert to Morocco, Performed in the Years 1824-1828 Vols. 1 and 2,* is available from *books.google.com/books?id=ex5OAAAAcAAJ&printsec=frontcover&dq=rene+Callié&hl=en&sa=X&ei=gqlpUbDQNYa08QTU5oGQBg&ved=0CEcQ6AEwBA#v=onepage&q=rene%20caillie&f=false.* His description of Timbuktu can be found in Vol. 2.

49. *Ibid.,* p. 49.

50. *Ibid.*, p. 83.

51. *Ibid.*, p. 64.

52. Note the language and imagery used to describe the Tuareg, this is representative of a colonial narrative that constructed a Tuareg identity that is still influential today. See Edward L. Bimberg, "Faceless Warriors of the Sahara," *Military History*, January/February 2006.

53. Martin Klein, *Slavery and Colonial Rule in French West Africa*, Cambridge, UK: Cambridge University Press, 1998, p. 139.

54. A. S. Kanya-Forstner, *The Conquest of the Western Sahara: A Study of French Military Imperialism*, Cambridge, UK: Cambridge University Press, 1969.

55. *Ibid.*

56. Francesca Davis Di Piazza, *Mali in Pictures*, Minneapolis, MN: Lerner Publishing, 2007.

57. Matthew Saltmarsh, "Colonial Soldiers Want more from France," *The New York Times,* August 12, 2009, available from *www.nytimes.com/2009/08/13/world/europe/13iht-vets.html?pagewanted=all&_r=0.*

58. John D. Hargreaves, *Decolonization in Africa*, London, UK: Longman, 1996.

59. Global Security, "Algerian National Liberation (1954-1962)," available from *www.globalsecurity.org/military/world/war/algeria.htm.*

60. Serge Berstein, *The Republic of De Gaulle 1958-1969*, Paris, France: Institut d'Etudes Politiques, 2006.

61. "France Remembers the Algerian War, 50 Years On," *France 24*, March 19, 2012, available from *www.france24.com/en/20120316-commemorations-mark-end-algerian-war-independence-france-evian-accords.*

62. Many French colonies achieved independence in 1960: Benin, Togo, Burkina Faso, Mauritania, Niger, Gabon, Ivory Coast, and Chad.

63. William J. Foltz, *From French West Africa to the Mali Federation*, New Haven, CT: Yale University Press, 1965.

64. *Ibid.*, p. 189.

65. Robert Pringle, "Miracle in Mali," *The Wilson Quarterly*, Vol. 30, No. 2, 2006, pp. 31-39, available from *www.wilsonquarterly.com/essays/miracle-in-mali*.

66. Susanna D. Wing, *Constructing Democracy in Africa: Mali in Transition*, New York: Palgrave Macmillan, 2008, p. 8.

67. The Malian constitution limits the president to two 5-year terms.

68. Robert Pringle, "Democratization in Mali: Putting History to Work," Washington, DC: U.S. Institutes of Peace, 2006, p. 1.

69. "Mali President Touré Resigns in Deal with Coup Leaders," BBC, April 8, 2012, available from *www.bbc.co.uk/news/world-africa-17653882*.

70. L. Diarra and H. Breman, "The Influence of Rainfall on the Productivity of Grasslands" in *Evaluation and Mapping of Tropical African Rangelands, Proceedings of the Seminar 3-6 March 1975, Bamako Mali*, International Livestock Centre for Africa, Ethiopia, 1975.

71. Population figures are estimates and based on the *CIA World Factbook*, Tuaregs make up approximately 10 percent of population in Mali and Niger.

72. H. T. Norris, *The Tuaregs: Their Islamic Legacy and Diffusion in the Sahel*, Warminster (UK): Aris & Phillips, 1975.

73. *Ibid.*

74. Minority Rights Group International, *World Directory of Minorities and Indigenous Peoples – Mali: Overview*, 2007, available from *www.refworld.org/docid/4954ce5bc.html*.

75. Robert Pringle, "Democratization in Mali: Putting History to Work," Washington DC: U.S. Institutes of Peace, 2006.

76. Mali's neighbors, Burkina Faso, Chad, and Niger, are ranked 183, 184, and 186, respectively. See "Mali Country Profile: Human Development Indicators," available from *hdrstats.undp.org/en/countries/profiles/MLI.html*.

77. World Bank, "Mali."

78. The total fertility rate is the average number of children born to a woman over her lifetime. This figure is typically reported at the country level.

79. World Bank, "Mali Overview."

80. Wieteke Aster Holthuijzen and Jacqueline Rugaimukamu Maximillian, "Dry, Hot, and Brutal: Desertification in the Sahel of Mali," *Journal of Sustainable Development in Africa*, Vol. 13, No. 7, 2011, pp. 245-268, available from *www.jsd-africa.com/Jsda/Vol13No7-Winter2011A/PDF/Dry%20Hot%20and%20Brutal.Wieteke%20Holthuijzen.pdf*.

81. "Shaping Climate-Resilient Development: A Framework for Decision-Making," Economics of Climate Adaption Working Group, 2009.

82. Scott Baldauf, "Mali Moves Music Festival as Tourism Threatened by AQ Threat," *The Christian Science Monitor*, January 8, 2010, available from *www.csmonitor.com/World/Africa/2010/0108/Mali-moves-music-festival-as-tourism-threatened-by-Al-Qaeda-threat/(page)/2*.

83. "Mali Kidnapping: One Dead and Three Seized in Timbuktu," BBC, November 25, 2011, available from *www.bbc.co.uk/news/world-africa-15895908*.

84. Tom Pryor, "Festival in the Desert Announces 2013 Plans," *The National Geographic Magazine*, October 23, 2012, available from

*worldmusic.nationalgeographic.com/view/page.basic/article/content.
article/festival_in_the_desert_2013/en_US.*

85. Pringle, "Democratization in Mali."

86. Kalifa Keita, "Conflict and Conflict Resolution in the Sahel: The Tuareg Insurgency in Mali," Carlisle, PA: Strategic Studies Institute, U.S. Army War College, 1998.

87. Pringle, "Democratization in Mali."

88. Keita, pp. 10-11.

89. Lutz Barend, "Tuareg desert blues, rebellions and music festivals," September, 11, 2012, Africa Interpreted' blog by Consultancy Africa Intelligence (CAI), available from *consultancy africablog.com/2012/09/11/tuareg-desert-blues-rebellions-and-music-festivals/*.

90. Klaus M. Leisinger and Karin Schmitt, *Survival in the Sahel: An Ecological and Developmental Challenge*, The Hague, The Netherlands: International Service for National Agricultural Research, 1995.

91. Peter Gwin, "Mali: How Al Qaeda Claimed Timbuktu," Pulitzer Center for Crisis Reporting. December 12, 2012, available from *pulitzercenter.org/reporting/timbuktu-al-qaeda-mali-libya-tuareg-Qaddafi-mercenaries-obama-arab-spring-economy-tourism-terrorism.*

92. Andy Morgan, "The Causes of the Uprising in Northern Mali," *Think Africa Press*, April 6, 2012, available from *thinkafricapress.com/mali/causes-uprising-northern-mali-tuareg.*

93. R. Poulton and I. ag.Youssouf, *A Peace of Timbuktu: Democratic Governance, Development and African Peacemaking*, Geneva, Switzerland: United Nations Institute for Disarmament Research, 1998.

94. Wing, p. 160.

95. "National Pact Concluded Between the Government of Mali and the Unified Movements and Fronts of Azawad Giving Expression to the Special Status of Northern Mali," April 1, 11, 992, available from *https://peaceaccords.nd.edu/site_media/media/accords/Mali_Peace_Accord-proof.pdf*.

96. Keita, p. 18.

97. Morgan.

98. Ag Bahanga died on August 26, 2011.

99. Ferdaous Bouhlel-Hardy, Yvan Guichaoua and Abdoulaye Tamboura, "Tuareg Crisis in Niger and Mali," Paris, France: Ifri, 2007.

100. "Strife in the Sahel: A Perfect Desert Storm," *The Economist.* March 17, 2012.

101. "Ex-Gaddafi Tuareg Fighters Boost Mali Rebels," *BBC News Africa*, October 17, 2011.

102. "Putting Mali Back on the Constitutional Track," Dakar, Senegal/Brussels, Belgium: International Crisis Group, March 26, 2012, available from *www.crisisgroup.org/en/publication-type/alerts/2012/mali-putting-mali-back-on-the-constitutional-track.aspx*.

103. Drew Hinshaw, "Mali Rebels Add Timbuktu to Areas in Their Control," *The Wall Street Journal*, April 1, 2012.

104. Robyn Dixon and Jane Labous, "Gains of Mali's Tuareg Rebels Appear Permanent, Analysts Say," *The Los Angeles Times*, April 4, 2012.

105. Horand Knaup, "Fighting in Mali Adds Chaos to Troubled African Region," *Spiegel Online International*, May 11, 2012.

106. International Crisis Group.

107. Poulton and Ag Youssouf.

108. Scott Stewart, "Mali Besieged by Fighters Fleeing Libya," *Stratfor*, February 2, 2012, available from *www.stratfor.com/weekly/ mali-besieged-fighters-fleeing-libya*.

109. "Strife in the Sahel."

110. Andrew Chuter, "5,000 Libyan MANPADS Secured," *Defense News*. April, 12, 2012.

111. "Strife in the Sahel."

112. Lesley Anne Warner, "Instability in Mali Complicates Regional Approach to AQIM," *World Politics Review*, April 5, 2012, p. 1-1.

113. Stewart; P. Batacchi, "Tuaregs Seized Regional Zeitgeist in Successful Coup," *Defense News*, April 22, 2012.

114. *Ibid.*

115. Peter Dorrie, "Mali's Tuareg Rebellion Puts Region at Risk," *World Politics Review*, March 14, 2012.

116. Jonathan Masters, "Al Qaeda in the Islamic Maghreb (AQIM)," *Council on Foreign Relations*, 2013, available from *www. cfr.org/north-africa/al-qaeda-islamic-maghreb-aqim/p12717*.

117. Review of the documents seized in Bin Laden's Abbottabad compound by the Harmony Program at the Combatting Terrorism Center (CTC) at West Point found that the discussions related to AQIM "were not substantive enough to inform an understanding of the relationship between AQiM and al Qai'da's senior leadership and these groups." See Nelly Lahoud, Stuart Caudill, Liam Collins, Gabriel Koehler-Derrick, Don Rassler, and Muhammad al 'Ubayti, "Letters from Abbottabad: Bin Laden Sidelined?" May 3, 2012, West Point, New York: CTC.

118. For a more comprehensive list of attacks, see John Rollins, "Al Qaeda and its Affiliates: Historical Perspective, Global Presence and Implications for U.S. Policy," Washington, DC: Congressional Research Service, January 25, 2011.

119. Erin Foster-Bowser and Angelia Saunders, "Security Threats in the Sahel and Beyond: AQIM, Boko Haram, and al Shabaab," Norfolk, VA: Civil Military Fusion Centre (NATO), April 2012, available from *www.cimicweb.org/cmo/medbasin/Holder/Documents/r013%20CFC%20Monthly%20Thematic%20Report%20(18-APR-12).pdf*.

120. See also Knaup, 2012.

121. Geoff D. Porter, "AQIM's Objectives in North Africa," *CTC Sentinel*, February 1, 2011, available available from *www.ctc.usma.edu/posts/aqim%E2%80%99s-objectives-in-north-africa*.

122. John Rollins, *Al Qaeda and Affiliates: A Historical Perspective, Global Presence and Implications for U.S. Policy*, Washington DC: Congressional Research Service, January 25, 2011, p. 20.

123. Batacchi.

124. Stewart, 2012.

125. "Strife in the Sahel."

126. *Ibid*.

127. Norman Cigar, and Stephanie E. Kramer, eds., "Al-Qaida After Ten Years of War: A Global Perspective of Success, Failure and Prospects," Washington, DC: U.S. Government Printing Office, March 30, 2012; and Modibo Goita, "West Africa's Growing Terrorist Threat from Confronting AQIM's Sahelian Strategy," *Africa Security Brief*, Washington, DC: Africa Center for Strategic Studies, National Defense University, 2011.

128. Raby Ould Idoumou, "AQIM Fighters impose Sharia in Gao," *Maghrebia*, July 4, 2012, available from *magharebia.com/en_GB/articles/awi/features/2012/07/04/feature-03?change_locale=true*.

129. Andrew Lebovich, "AQIM and its allies in Mali," Washington, DC: The Washington Institute, February 5, 2013, available from *www.washingtoninstitute.org/policy-analysis/view/aqim-and-its-allies-in-mali*.

130. Dixon and Labous.

131. International Crisis Group, 2012.

132. William Lloyd-George, "Armed Groups in Northern Mali Raping Women," IPS Inter Press Service, April 24, 2012, available from *www.ips.org/africa/2012/04/armed-groups-in-northern-mali-raping-women/*.

133. "Ansar al-Din, MNLA Sign Deal in Algiers," *Maghrebia*, December 23, 2012.

134. "Strange Bedfellows: The MNLAs On-Again, Off-Again Marriage with Ansar Dine," *France 24*, June 27, 2012, available from *www.france24.com/en/20120605-mali-strange-bedfellows-mnla-ansar-dine-al-qaeda-aqim-islamists-tuareg*.

135. "Tuareg Forces Ready to Help French Forces in Mali," *Al Arabiya News*, January 14, 2013, available from *www.alarabiya.net/articles/2013/01/14/260337.html*.

136. Foster-Bowser and Saunders.

137. "Mali Islamists Claim Menaka Victory Against Rebels," BBC News, November 19, 2012, available from *www.bbc.co.uk/news/world-africa-20404519*.

138. "UN Security Council Approves Mali Intervention Force," *AFP*, December 21, 2012, available from *www.afp.com/en/news/topstories/un-security-council-approves-mali-intervention-force*.

139. "France Goes it Alone," *The Economist*, January 14, 2013, available from *www.economist.com/blogs/charlemagne/2013/01/french-foreign-policy*.

140. "Heavy Casualties in Northern Mali Fighting," *Al Jazeera*, February 23, 2013, available from *www.aljazeera.com/news/africa/2013/02/201322223819792689.html*.

141. Jorge Bentiz, "The Cost of the French Mission in Mali: Operation Serval," NATO Source Alliance News Blog, April 26, 2013.

142. "U.S. Spy Drones Aiding in Mali Conflict," UPI, March 4, 2013, available from *www.upi.com/Top_News/World-News/2013/03/04/US-spy-drones-aiding-Mali-conflict/UPI-40421362411298/*.

143. Craig Whitlock, "Pentagon Deploys Small Number of Troops to War-Torn Mali," *The Washington Post*, April 30, 2103, available from *articles.washingtonpost.com/2013-04-30/world/38921208_1_robert-firman-mali-bamako*.

144. Adam Entous, "U.S. Agrees to Support French in Mali with Plane Refueling," *The Wall Street Journal*, January 27, 2013, available from *online.wsj.com/article/SB10001424127887324039504578266893897303204.html*.

145. David Pugliese, "Canadian Forces Mission to Mali 'Ends with a Bit of Whimper'," *The Ottawa Citizen*, April 18, 2013.

146. "Mali Crisis: French Troops Begin Withdrawal," BBC, April 9, 2013, available from *www.bbc.co.uk/news/world-africa-22079290*.

147. Security Council Report, "Mali: April 2013 Monthly Forecast," March 28, 2013, available from *www.securitycouncilreport.org/monthly-forecast/2013-04/mali_6.php*.

148. *Ibid.; Mali April 2013 Monthly Forecast.*

149. Princeton N. Lyman and J. Stephen Morrison, "The Terrorist Threat in Africa," *Foreign Affairs*, Vol. 83, Issue 1, January/February 2004, pp. 75-86.

150. Donna Miles, "New Counterterrorism Initiative to Focus on Southern Africa," *Armed Forces Press Service*, May 17, 2005, available from *www.eucom.mil/article/21641/New-counterterrorism-initiative-focus-Saharan*.

151. Craig Whitlock, "Taking Terror Fight to North Africa Leads U.S. to Unlikely Alliances," *The Washington Post*, October 28, 2006, available from *www.washingtonpost.com/wp-dyn/content/article/2006/10/27/AR2006102701713.html*.

152. Lianne Kennedy Boudali, "The Trans-Sahara Counterterrorism Partnership," West Point, NY: United States Military Academy, The Combating Terrorism Center, April, 2007, available from *www.dtic.mil/cgi-bin/GetTRDoc?AD=ADA466542*.

153. Miles.

154. "Flintlock 2012 Exercise Postponed," Bamako, Mali: Embassy of the United States, available from *mali.usembassy.gov/flint-lock_2012_posponed.html*.

155. "10 Things about Atlas Accord 2012," February 24, 2012, AFRICOM Blog, available from *africom.wordpress. com/2012/02/24/10-things-about-atlas-accord-2012/*.

156. "President Bush Creates a Department of Defense Unified Combatant Command for Africa," Washington, DC: The White House, February 6, 2007, available from *georgewbush-white-house.archives.gov/news/releases/2007/02/20070206-3.html*.

157. Robert G. Berschinski, *AFRICOM's Dilemma: The "Global War on Terrorism," "Capacity Buiiding," "Humanitarianism" and the Future of U.S. Security Policy*, Carlisle, PA: The U.S. Army War College, 2007, available from *www.strategicstudiesinstitute.army. mil/pdffiles/pub827.pdf*.

158. J. Stephen Morrison, Mark Bellamy, and Kathleen Hicks, "Strengthening AFRICOM's Case," Washington, DC: Center for Strategic and International Studies, March 5, 2008, available from *csis.org/publication/strengthening-africoms-case-0*.

159. David Gutelius, "U.S. Creates African Enemies Where None Were Before," *The Christian Science Monitor*, July 11, 2003, available from *www.csmonitor.com/2003/0711/p11s01-coop.html*.

160. Testimony of Dr. David Gutelius Partner, Ishtirak Consulting Senior Fellow, Johns Hopkins University Applied Physics Laboratory, Before The Senate Committee on Foreign Relations Subcommittee on African Affairs, "Examining U.S. Counterterrorism Priorities and Strategies Across Africa's Sahel Region," November 17, 2009, available from *www.foreign.senate.gov/imo/ media/doc/GuteliusTestimony091117a1.pdf*.

161. Josephine Osikena, "Africa's Alternative Security and Development Partnerships," in David J. Francis, ed., U.S. *Strategy in Africa: AFRICOM, Terrorism and Security Challenges*, London, UK: Routledge, 2010. Complete copy of NEPAD Framework Statement available from *www.nepad.org/system/files/NEPAD%20 Framework%20(English).pdf.*

162. Warner, p. 1.

163. John Irish and Daniel Flynn, "Chad Emerges as African Power Broker as France Steps Back," *Reuters,* May 8, 2013, available from *ca.reuters.com/article/topNews/idCABRE94707C20130508.*

164. Bakari Gueye, "Mauritanian Army Boosts Border Presence," *Magharebia,* April 12, 2012.

165. *Special Operations Forces Operating Concept,* McDill Air Force Base, FL: U.S. Southern Command (USSOCOM), May 2013.

166. Dona J. Stewart: "The Greater Middle East in the Bush Administration's Ideological Imagination," *The Geographical Review,* Vol. 95, No. 3, July 2005, pp. 400-424.

167. "The Middle East Partnership Initiative: Promoting Democratization in a Troubled Region," Hearing before the Subcommittee on the Middle East and Central Asia of the Committee on International Relations, House of Representatives, 108th Cong., 1st Sess., March 19, 2003, available from *commdocs.house.gov/committees/intlrel/hfa85842.000/hfa85842_0f.htm.*

168. Laurence Aida Ammour, "Regional Security Cooperation in the Maghreb and the Sahel: Algeria's Pivotal Ambivalence," *Africa Security Brief,* No. 13, February 2012.

169. "Mali: The Need for Determined and Coordinated International Action," Washington DC: International Crisis Group, September 24, 2012.

170. Walid Ramzi, "Algeria Freezes Mali Military Support," *Magharebia,* January 31, 2012, available from *www.magharebia.com/ cocoon/awi/xhtml1/en _GB/features/2012/01/31/feature-02.*

171. Stewart, 2012.

172. Miguel Hernando De Larramendi, "Intra-Maghreb Relations: Unitary Myth and National Interests," in Yahia H. Zoubir and Hazam Amirah-Fernandez, *North Africa Politics, Region and the Limits of Transformation*, London, UK: Routledge, 2008.

173. Maxime Larive, "France in War: Operation Serval," Foreign Policy Association Blog, January 16, 2013, available from *foreignpolicyblogs.com/2013/01/16/france-in-war-operation-serval/*.

174. Ammour, based on 2010 figures from "Armaments, Disarmaments and International Security," *Stockholm International Peace Research Institute (SIPRI) Yearbook 2010*, Stockholm, Sweden: SIPRI, 2010; and *The Military Balance 2010*, London, UK: International Institute for Strategic Studies, 2010.

175. Lesley Anne Warner, "Instability in Mali Complicates Regional Approach to AQIM," *World Politics Review*, April, 5, 2012, p. 1-1.

176. Ammour.

177. "Algeria Gains Crucial Help in the Fight Against Al Qaeda," *The New York Times*, November 3, 2012, available from *www.nytimes.com/2012/11/04/world/africa/algeria-gains-berber-help-in-pushing-out-al-qaeda.html?_r=0*.

178. Tyrone Marshall, "AFRICOM Commander Addresses Concerns, Potential Solutions in Mali," *American Forces Press Service*, January 24, 2013, available from *www.africom.mil/Newsroom/Article/10234/general-ham-at-howard-university*.

179. Matthew Redding, "Mali: The Importance of SSR in Bamako," Waterloo, Ontario, Canada: Security Sector Reform Resource Center, January 9, 2013, available from *www.ssrresourcecentre.org/2013/01/09/mali-the-importance-of-ssr-in-bamako/*.

180. "Crisis Warning on North Africa," *The Wall Street Journal*, April 10, 2012.

181. *Ibid.*

182. Foreign Area Office, April 2012, p. 1.

183. Dorrie.

184. "Mali Crisis, Situation Report No. 12," The World Food Programme, March 8, 2013, available from *home.wfp.org/stellent/groups/public/documents/ep/wfp255935.pdf.*

185. United Nations High Commissioner for Refugees (UNHCR), "Operation Mali," available from *data.unhcr.org/MaliSituation/regional.php.*

186. "Mali Food Security Outlook Update," FEWS — Famine Early Warning Systems Network, May 2013, available from *reliefweb.int/sites/reliefweb.int/files/resources/Mali%20Food%20Security%20Outlook%20Update%20May%202013.pdf.*

187. "The World Bank, "Mali Overview," available from *www.worldbank.org/en/country/mali/overview.*

188. Rob Bailey, "Food Crisis in West Africa: Action Needed," London, UK: Chatham House, December 9, 2011.

189. "WFP at the Forefront of Response to Complex Emergency in Mali, Bamako," World Food Programme, March 23, 2012, available from *www.wfp.org/stories/wfp-forefront-response-complex-emergency-mali.*

190. Wieteke Aster Holthuijzen and Jacqueline Rugaimukamu Maximillian, "Dry, Hot and Brutal: Desertification in the Sahel of Mali," *Journal of Sustainable Development in Africa*, Vol. 13, No. 7, 2011, pp. 245-268, available from *www.jsd-africa.com/Jsda/Vol13No7-Winter2011A/PDF/Dry%20Hot%20and%20Brutal.Wieteke%20Holthuijzen.pdf.*

191. "Shaping Climate-Resilient Development: A Framework for Decision-Making, "Report of the Economics of Climate Adaptation Working Group," San Francisco, CA: Climate Works Foundation, 2009, available from *ccsl.iccip.net/climate_resilient.pdf.*

192. "Mali Rebels Launch Guerrilla Attack on Gao," *Al Jazeera*, February 11, 2013.

193. "Two Malian soldiers killed in suicide attack near Gao," *British Broadcasting Corporation*, May 4, 2013, available from *www.bbc.co.uk/news/world-africa-22416987*.

194. "The Al-Qaida Papers - Drones."

195. Adam Nossiter, "Mali's Prime Minister Resigns After Arrest, Mudding Plans to Retake the North," *The New York Times*, December 12, 2012.

196. "Keita Wins Mali Polle as Cissé Concedes Defeat," *France 24*, August 13, 2013; and Daniel Flynn and Tiemoko Diallo, "Front-runner in Mali Election Runoff Pledges to Reinforce Peace," *Reuters*, August 9, 2013.

197. Lydia Polgreen, "Islamists' Harsh Rule Awakens Ethnic Tensions in Mali," *The New York Times*, February 17, 2013.

198. Flynn and Diallo.

199. Heather Hurlburt, "Mali's Crisis Caused by Development Failures, Not Military Aid," *The Guardian*, January 15, 2013.

www.ingramcontent.com/pod-product-compliance
Lightning Source LLC
Chambersburg PA
CBHW070259290526
45791CB00003B/1007